W9-AQN-991

EDGAR FAWCETT

Twayne's United States Authors Series

Sylvia E. Bowman, *Editor*

INDIANA UNIVERSITY

Edgar Fawcett

EDGAR FAWCETT

By STANLEY R. HARRISON

Mansfield State College

 201

Twayne Publishers, Inc.   ::   New York

Copyright © 1972 by Twayne Publishers, Inc.

All Rights Reserved

Library of Congress Catalog Card Number: 74-161801

818.4
F278H

MANUFACTURED IN THE UNITED STATES OF AMERICA

To Jenny and Sam

and

For Stanley Dionysius—the Egger was always for him

84889

84888

Preface

It is fascinating to speculate upon the origins of creative motivation because the initial impulses are forever shifting and cloaked in shadow. In fact, the tremors that prompt the artistic urge are so enveloped in mystique and so imbedded in the individual psyche that the psychologist and the biographer have been intrigued by the fascination of such studies and, in recent years, have joined forces with the literary scholar in an attempt to illuminate first causes. Perhaps, however, their collective efforts have been pointless; for it is more than likely that John Milton touched upon the sensitive nerve of creation in *Lycidas* when he intuited that "fame is the spur."

For the writer, fame is indeed the spur, a most highly prized and elusive desire that is granted to few; adverse judgment and the passing of time soon cast scores of others into a literary wasteland. The psychologist passes over the lesser known writer—in fact, he does not even know of his existence—in his haste to probe the mind and works of the more successful author; the biographer, too, focuses upon the writer of repute—it is almost as if he cannot conceive of there being anything of interest in the life of the minor literary figure; and the literary historian traces his traditions from major figure to major figure with little regard for the role played by the obscure writer in the development of tradition.

The slight paid the author of limited range and depth is intellectually understandable; but, curiously enough, it is also intellectually unpardonable. The same internal passions and psychic tremors that impel the literary master also mark the behavior of the less talented writer and make him equally as fit a subject for analytic study. In fact, he is probably a more curious psychological phenomenon upon the literary scene, for failure seldom diminishes his ardor; it rather inflames it. The external actions of the writer, which inevitably attract the biographer, must differ considerably from lesser to greater light, but, then, they do also from individual to individual, and biographies of determination and frustration are every bit as absorbing as those of effort and fulfillment.

When literary historians pay scant attention to the minor writer or ignore him completely, they overlook the part he plays in keeping tradition alive; they fail to see the pioneering role he often assumes in charting new literary directions; and they blind themselves to the vibrating nature of influence studies, for often the major figure influences the minor one, who, in turn, exerts his sway upon countless others. Thus, our minor author, in his own way, may be as significant to the study of literature as our writer of the first rank. Such a minor figure was Edgar Fawcett, whose Realistic and Naturalistic novels in the latter part of the nineteenth century played a vital role in the literary movement that proved to be the breeding ground for the works of Hamlin Garland, Stephen Crane, Frank Norris, Jack London, and Theodore Dreiser, and whose international novels, strongly influenced by Henry James, occupied a place of some significance in the development of this particular American literary tradition.

Ever since the creation of the History of Ideas Club at Johns Hopkins University in 1923, a small group of scholars have been searching for men like Edgar Fawcett—representative men whose writings illuminate the political, social, philosophical, scientific, and literary tendencies of an age. Fawcett was to the close of the nineteenth century what, in Crane Brinton's opinion, Sir Walter Scott and Robert Southey were to the early years of the same century. Brinton, confining his remarks to the political thought of the English Romantics, maintained that:

Men like Scott and Southey . . . were politically very close to the average plain citizen. Like most men they did not create their political standards, but took them from circumstances, from leaders and thinkers, from the spirit of the age. . . . You will find among them neither a Creevey nor a Kant. They look at the political scene from an angle quite their own; but it is an angle that much more nearly coincides with that from which the vast inarticulate mass of spectators sees it than any of which we have a consistent record.[1]

Fawcett's novels, essays, poems, and plays offer an insight into the political corruption of his age, a commentary upon the existence of a plutocracy within a democratic nation, a feeling for the confusion created by new philosophical concepts, and a reaction to the consequences of scientific learning and progress. His works also provide a rare insight into the origin, philosophy, and esthetic development of literary Realism and Naturalism and a significant view of the international theme in American literature, as well they might, since these literary movements were themselves outgrowths of the wider intellectual currents of the time.

Despite Fawcett's feeling for his era, literary obscurity came quickly to him. His output was so vast during his lifetime that George Parsons Lathrop, writing in the November, 1886, issue of *Harper's Magazine*, remarked that Fawcett "has been before the public for fifteen years, and during that period he has been more prolific both of verse and prose than any of his fellows among local authors." [2] Yet William H. Rideing, in an article in the *Bookman*, in December, 1910, only six years after Fawcett's death, when commenting upon the fleeting nature of literary fame and popularity, said: "Take Edgar Fawcett, for instance. Speak of him to readers below middle age now, and you will find that they know nothing of him. Thirty years ago he was a celebrity and one of the best known figures in New York, a man familiar about town as well as in literary circles, from whom came a steady flow of plays, novels and books of verse, all of which attracted attention, though opinion as to their merit conflicted and ran to extremes." [3]

Edgar Fawcett was probably one of the most prolific of all American writers; he was certainly the most versatile in his writing of two verse dramas, seven volumes of poetry, some seventy novels, five stage plays that were produced, plus innumerable essays, critical articles, and short stories.[4] The volume of his publication is in itself impressive and so are some of the judgments passed upon his writing in his own time. William Dean Howells, for one, said of Fawcett that, as a poet of Fancy, he was the "first . . . among all the English-writing poets of our time." [5] Fame, however, remains elusive; and failure emerges as a thing of complexity. Failure is never one-dimensional, and there will be no attempt to simplify it here, but rather, through an analysis of Fawcett's published writings, to call attention to its sporadic manifestations of excellence, to appreciate its significances, and to understand why it overtook the man whose literary works gained the respect of Thomas Bailey Aldrich,[6] John Greenleaf Whittier,

James Russell Lowell, William Dean Howells, Hamlin Garland, Oscar Wilde, and Henry James.

Edgar Fawcett was not a great writer—he is not for all time—but he was of an age; and our understanding of the literary directions, the critical controversies, and the intellectual currents of that age is considerably enriched for his having created his art out of the fabric of his time.

I would like to thank the United States Trust Company of New York for granting me the rights to the Fawcett letters and to express my appreciation to the libraries that have given me permission to reprint them. Excerpts from the Fawcett letters appear by courtesy of the Trustees of the Boston Public Library, the Chicago Historical Society, the Columbia University Library, the Cornell University Library, the Duke University Library, the Henry E. Huntington Library and Art Gallery, the New York Public Library, the State University of New York at Buffalo Library, the University of Southern California Library, and the Clifton Waller Barrett Library of the University of Virginia Library.

Contents

Chronology

1847   Edgar Fawcett born, May 26.

1867   Graduated from Columbia College in New York City.

1870   Received master's degree from Columbia College.

1871   First novel, *Asses Ears*.

1872   *Short Poems for Short People*.

1873   *Purple and Fine Linen*.

1876   *Ellen Story*.

1878   *Fantasy and Passion* (poetry).

1880   *A False Friend*, opened at Union Square Theater in New York, June 21; *Our First Families*, opened at Daly's Theater in New York, September 23; *The False Friend*, a novel adapted from the stage play; *A Hopeless Case*.

1881   *Sixes and Sevens*, opened at the Bijou Opera House in New York in March; *Americans Abroad*, opened at Daly's Theater in New York, October 5; *A Gentleman of Leisure*.

1884   *Adventures of a Widow; An Ambitious Woman; Rutherford; Tinkling Cymbals; The Buntling Ball; Song and Story, Later Poems*.

1885   *The New King Arthur; Social Silhouettes*.

1886   *Romance and Revery* (poetry).

1887   *The Earl*, opened at Hollis Street Theater in Boston, April 11; *The House at High Bridge; The Confessions of Claud*.

1888   *Divided Lives; Douglas Duane; A Man's Will; Miriam Balestier; Olivia Delaplaine*.

1889   *A Demoralizing Marriage; The Evil That Men Do; Solarion; Agnosticism and Other Essays; Blooms and Brambles* (poetry).

1890   *A Daughter of Silence; Fabian Dimitry; How a Husband Forgave*.

1891   *A New York Family; A Romance of Two Brothers; Women Must Weep; Songs of Doubt and Dream* (poetry).

1892   *The Adopted Daughter; American Push; An Heir to Millions*.

1893 *Loaded Dice; The New Nero.*
1894 *Her Fair Fame; A Martyr of Destiny; A Mild Barbarian; Outrageous Fortune.*
1895 *The Ghost of Guy Thyrle.*
1896 *Life's Fitful Fever.*
1897 Emigrated to England; *A Romance of Old New York; Two Daughters of One Race.*
1898 *New York.*
1903 *The Vulgarians; Voices and Visions, Later Verses.*
1904 *An Innocent Anglomaniac; The Pride of Intellect.*
Died in England, May 2.

CHAPTER *1*

Literary Life

E DGAR Fawcett was born in New York City on May 26, 1847.
From that time until his graduation from Columbia College
in 1867 and his subsequent emergence as a literary figure, relatively little is known about him. The entry in the *Dictionary of
American Biography* is typical of other biographical accounts of
these early years in that it contains a paucity of information: [1]

FAWCETT, EDGAR (May 26, 1847—May 2, 1904), author, was born
in New York, and despite much foreign travel and a residence abroad
during his later years, his native city remained throughout his life
the principal theme of his literary work. His father, Frederick Fawcett, was an Englishman who became a prosperous merchant in New
York; his mother, Sarah Lawrence Fawcett, was of American descent.
After obtaining his preliminary education in the public schools of
New York, Fawcett entered Columbia College. Here he failed of
distinction as a student—his name appeared on the minutes of faculty
meetings chiefly as the recipient of admonitions for irregular at-
tendance upon classes—but he gained a campus reputation as a man of
letters, and as a member of the Philolexian literature society, he was
prominent in undergraduate literary activities. He graduated in 1867,
and three years later Columbia conferred the degree of M.A. upon
him. [2]

By 1880, however, only ten years after receiving his master's
degree from Columbia, Fawcett had achieved sufficient literary
reputation to prompt an editorial sketch in the *New York Times,*
where he was described as being "of medium height, solidly,
though proportionately built, with a rather square head, dark eyes,
florid complexion, black hair and mustache." The description concluded with the observation that "he is so earnest in the pursuit of
literature that he hires a fourth-story room in a tenement house on

the East Side, where he may work without interruption. His love of manuscript-making must be an uncontrollable passion." [3]

And an uncontrollable passion it was. Fawcett's deep, personal involvement with literature was evident in his every word and action; he never tempered his emotional reaction with decorous platitude when literary judgment was at issue. He dismissed Josiah Holland as "a despicable literary figure," [4] and he characterized Richard Henry Stoddard as "a wretched, pathetic sort of figure." "As a poet," Fawcett wrote, "I have never thought Stoddard of the least consequence. As a man I begin to think him worthy of much greater contempt." [5] With the bluntness and honesty characteristic of him, Fawcett dismissed Sidney Lanier's verse because it "shocks, irritates & disgusts"; [6] and he insisted that Walt Whitman was nothing more than a "contumacious buffalo of letters." [7]

Even when remarking upon Alfred Tennyson, his favorite poet, Fawcett could not help but betray his intense literary concern and personal anguish: "By the way, 'Harold' is just announced here. I tremble for fear it may be some such senile stupidity as *Queen Mary*. Its 'dramatic form' has a very suspicious sound. I hope that I may not be called upon to say, at the end of this new poem, something relative to the advisability of Tennyson's immediate death. But what words am I speaking? 'Harold' *may* prove a masterpiece . . . and yet I somehow feel in my bones that I am going to gnash my teeth over it." [8]

The editorial writer for the *New York Times* divined this "uncontrollable passion" in Fawcett because it was unmistakably there. Fawcett's rooms, during the daylight hours, were always littered with books he had pulled from the shelves with abandon the previous evening. The works of Tennyson, John Keats, Algernon Swinburne, Charles Baudelaire, and Percy Bysshe Shelley were invariably on the floor, opened at the pages he loved to read, reread, and reread yet once more. His conversation with intimate friends, who were the minor literary figures of the time— Paul Hamilton Hayne, Frank Saltus, James Maurice Thompson, Julian Hawthorne, Thomas Bailey Aldrich—never strayed from literary affairs; and, when he was not talking literature, he was writing it. He seethed with ideas and wrote without letup. He always carried a writer's copybook with him, and the moment was rare that he was not entering his thoughts and observations in it. He created as he moved, no matter where the location, no matter what the condition. Once, within ten minutes of arriving at the top of the Righi in Switzerland, he composed a sonnet; another time he wrote a sonnet on Austerlitz while waiting to embark at Liverpool.[9]

This frenetic passion for literary creation did not suddenly erupt in Fawcett's mature years; he had nurtured the zeal since childhood. His own reminiscences reveal the early awakening of the literary impulse within:

In trying to recall just when I began to "write," I find myself drifting among very childish memories. Unless I greatly mistake, I could not have been much over nine years old when I conceived the idea of composing a story. I remember its name perfectly. I called it "Mrs. Morse; or, A Widow's Trials." At this time I had a mania for names, and on the first foolscap page of my maiden manuscript I placed eighteen, feminine and masculine. They designated the half-orphan progeny of my heroine, Mrs. Morse. She had been left with them at the opening of the tale, and she was supporting them (Walter, Olivia, Julian, Claribel, Harold, and thirteen others) under circumstances of the most poignant want. Their want was, indeed, so poignant that they were all stated to be in the early throes of starvation on my first foolscap page. Then I am distinctly conscious that I created a villain who held Mrs. Morse in her power, and who incidentally forced his way into her one miserable apartment and gloated over her. I had no conception of what I meant by letting my villain gloat. But it looked well, and I seemed to have some sort of authority for its being a tendency on the part of villains, so I introduced and rather simplified the circumstances. All the rest of the story is misted with forgetfulness, except one luridly dramatic point of it, near the close. One day, while Mrs. Morse, surrounded by her eighteen clinging children with their beautiful names, was being gloated upon more industriously than usual, the villain suddenly resolved to carry her off; but I feel certain that my unhappy Mrs. Morse accomplished her salvation by a *deus ex machina* which I thought singularly fine. Seizing a bottle of brandy, which by some blessed chance happened to be within arm's reach of this starving and prolific widow, she dexterously poured its contents down the villain's throat; and, while he was strangling from the results of this opportune alcoholic assault, Mrs. Morse eagerly followed by her enormous offspring, rushed from the clutches of her baffled tormentor. . . .

My future stories were all written in copy-books. And it is extraordinary how many copy bookfuls of fiction I produced during the next two years.[10]

The structure and character of Fawcett's works changed very little from these beginnings. He was as steeped in a nineteenth-century melodramatic tradition as ever was a William Dean Howells or a Thomas Hardy, and his plots were as complex and contrived as the best of Theodore Dreiser's novels. Accident and manipulation remained constant and became trademarks of Fawcett's later novels; the introduction of a villain or cynic—Adalbert Hurst, Austin Legree, Oscar Schuyler—was also an inevitable occurrence; and Fawcett's mania for names—Marmaduke Plinlimmon, Cyril Cursitor, Rivington Van Corlear—never abated. Of course, the voluminous production of Fawcett's early years never slackened either.

I *Failure*

Proliferation was the stamp of the man, but no matter what pleasure Fawcett may have derived from his productivity, he seldom had cause for satisfaction when he contemplated his reputation. He was constantly tormented by the thought that he was destined for literary obscurity. His correspondence with Paul Hamilton Hayne, though restrained in emotion, often reflected his despair. "To grasp the poetic spirit of our time is the most that any of us can do," he wrote in 1875. "Some do it very ill! I often believe myself among the number of bunglers!" One year later, in 1876, he wrote: "It seems to me that I have (pardon me) a rather strong *sense of words;* we have discussed this question before, you know, of my verbal coloring. Well, in the judgment of many, I suppose that to be this is merely to be mechanical or else turgid." Again, in 1876: "If I am ever really famous (and I never expect to be and care very little whether I am or no) your rosy prophecies shall be remembered." Finally, in December, 1878, Fawcett wrote that "I only wish . . . I could confine myself exclusively to one order of work, but I am compelled not alone to write poems and short stories, but novels as well. If I never come to anything—and I think the probability of my ultimate nothingness stronger every day—it will be solely because of this pressure; or so I imagine, but I may be wholly wrong here." [11]

In 1899, less than five years before his death, in a series of letters from London to Edmund Clarence Stedman, Fawcett, with a curious mixture of pride, acceptance, and irritation at an undeserved fate, expressed the same disappointment he had earlier conveyed to Hayne. Stedman had asked Fawcett's permission to include some of his poetry in a forthcoming anthology, and Fawcett responded:

If the American public does not think me worth purchasing in book-form—that is, the form I have assumed when addressing it—I greatly prefer not to be *à prendre ou à laisser* amid a crowd of lyrics &c. by other writers, even though these may be far and away my superiors. Since I have lived here several (not many, but several) requests for certain pieces of verse have come to me from strangers in course of preparing anthologies. I have always politely declined to allow them any use whatever of my compositions. No reasons appear to me quite justified. I have no position whatever before the American world of letters as a poet, and no one is more aware of that than your gifted father. I am perfectly willing to admit that I had not the note of distinction which deserved to be accepted by any large body of my cultured country-folk. But, nevertheless, facts like these, I should say, are not inconsistent with a wish to preserve what I hold an attitude of permissible dignity and reserve. I am no longer young, and a good while ago literary obscurity lost all terrors for me.

Stedman wrote again, but Fawcett was adamant:

Your letter is very kind, but it does not alter my views. I am wholly indifferent to but one thing, as regards my verse in America. That thing is my own indifference, or rather the chance of manifesting it, of exploiting it, whenever such a chance may arrive. All through the best years of my life they stamped upon me, jumped upon me . . . and now they have their reward—they have killed me. *Non omnis moriar,*[12] however, in at least one sense: they shall not read me in anthologies—not even in one so excellent and so far above the average as that which your scholarly hand is sure to make.[13]

Fawcett's alternating currents of pride and self-pity, evident in the letters to Stedman, also mark the character of Ralph Indermaur and his son, Kenneth, in *The Pride of Intellect,* Fawcett's last novel.[14] The career of the Indermaurs closely parallels Fawcett's; and their confessions in the novel, most assuredly of autobiographical implication, suggest that it was a lack of critical recognition, coupled with a sense of his own literary worth, that

prompted Fawcett to quit the United States in 1897. The elder
Indermaur dies, firmly convinced that his failure was a matter of
integrity and that his novels were superior to the critics who
judged them:

I have wanted you to swim with the current. I swam against it. I
was right; I shall die protesting I was right. But what is it, after all,
to be "Right"? One doesn't lose one's own soul—to put it fancifully—
but one misses the whole world. And to miss the whole world has
a prodigious meaning. If I were you, Kenneth, I would make "Propi-
tiate" my motto. Meet folk a little more than half way. Never cringe,
but constantly unbend. Whenever you discern a hate give it prompt
battle. That is, try and turn it into a friendship. Of all professions
the literary is most infested by hate. There, you see, the great prizes
are so few, the paths of ascent so craggy and thorny. There, too,
fashions are peculiarly despotic, and the levity of mere whim can
hurt like the blow of a bludgeon.[15]

It is a relatively simple matter to be made aware of the world's
judgment; it is altogether something else to accept it—and Fawcett's letters reveal that he did not. He held others responsible
for the miscarriage of his reputation. He often argued that insensitive publishers, in the throes of an unsettled market, vitiated
the strength of his writings by making capitulation to their taste
a condition of publication; at other times, he attributed his difficulties to the conservative desires of a reading public that was not
yet ready to accept his advanced views; most frequently, however,
he maintained that the critics, with their intolerable carping,
made a mockery of his intentions. There is a great deal of validity
in Fawcett's contentions, and his comments upon the publishers,
the reading public, and the critics suggest the extent of it.

II *The Publishers Versus the Writer*

If Fawcett ever paused in his assault upon the critics and the
reading public, it was not because he wearied of the crusade—
he loved it—but because he was otherwise occupied in attacking
the publishers. He had cause, he felt, to believe that primitive
publishing conditions and insensitive bookmen were partially
responsible for his uncertain literary fortunes. The matter of
royalties, for example, and contractual arrangements with pub-

lishers greatly disturbed and discouraged him. "I am disheart-
ened," Fawcett wrote to Hayne, "by the very thought of publishing my poems in this country. It seems to me that if Chatto and
Windus or Blackwood, in London, should bring them out, there
might be some vague chance for them; but here I doubt if 2000
copies would be sold—a miserable sale enough when our paltry
10 p.c. is considered, but a splendid one on the other side of
the water, where the author receives ½ profits. I almost think
that I will keep the poems till I can afford to go to England." [16]

For one reason or another, too many factors militated against
even a moderate financial success. Frank Luther Mott, in *Golden
Multitudes*, records that, during the period from 1875 to 1893,
book publishers were making smaller and smaller profits; greater
numbers of books were being placed at the mercy of bargain
seekers; and the quality of bookmaking was sinking to new and
lower depths. Mott attributes all of this decline to the emergence
of the dime novel and to the introduction of a cheap-book publishing program that resulted in a glutted and inactive market.[17]
Of this situation, Fawcett wrote to Bayard Taylor in 1878: "By
the way, the Messrs. Roberts pleasantly tell me that it will be
like burying the book to bring it out with the market in such a
slothful state; so I must of course bid goodbye to any thoughts
of a *succès d'argent*."[18]

Unsatisfactory royalty arrangements and an uncertain market
were only two unhappy conditions that the writer of Fawcett's
time had to overcome; editorial carelessness was a third. Fawcett
was a perfectionist. A work never left his hands until he had
developed it to its finest and most exact expression, and he raged
when the meaning of his work was distorted by the barbarisms
of a printer. In a letter from England, he wrote that "I am intensely sensitive to bad punctuation, & see that 'Keely' is full of
commas which I didn't place there. In the *1st* stanza there is one,
there are 3 in third & one in fourth. I take for granted that this
is the printer's work, but it makes nonsense of the text. For
instance, a comma after *nil de mortuis* is meaningless, or, rather,
destructive of meaning." [19]

Editorial revision was also destructive of content and meaning
on occasion. "Once," Fawcett complained, "I contributed a serial
story to The Youth's Companion' *[sic]* called 'The Country
Cousin'; but I did not offer it afterward to a publisher because

the *Y.C.* people changed my text at the end of the last chapter
in a way that I found very unsatisfactory." [20] And editorial prun-
ing was the most damaging publisher's weapon of all:

Roberts Bros have finally decided to bring out my poems, "Fantasy
& Passion," some time in early January. I say "my poems," but the
book has been cut down to 210 pages or thereabout, for imperative
reasons of saleability. "Hypocrites" & not a few of my cynical morbid
poems must be left out in this book, and oh! (a far harder thing to
bear) my three longest poems, "Alan Eliot," "Vanity of Vanities" and
"The Magic Flower" must also be postponed till another volume
appears—if it ever does appear! You may readily believe that I re-
belled against these Lycurgan decrees; but there was no appeal. I feel
as if 'Fantasy and Passion" had all the "passion" now taken out of it.
My "Hamlet," so to speak, has no Danish prince. "Fidelitas" remains
and not a few poems of that sort. There will perhaps be abt 200
poems in all. The idea is to make something picturesque and warm-
colored, without anything but an occasional shiver in it. Now I have
as dark a wrong side as I have a gay right; & this does not at all
please me, since I wished to publish a representative book of abt
350 pages and show the world at one *coup* what I am worth. Then, if
the world had shrugged its shoulders I should at least have had the
satisfaction of feeling that I had forcibly pulled its sleeve in my
effort to gain its notice. But Roberts was afraid of such a book, from
a commercial point of view, & I daresay that he is immensely right.[21]

Fawcett's bitterness toward publishers was deeply ingrained.
He frequently attributed his failures to their insensitive editing;
but, in a letter to a publisher, Paine, he expanded the reasons
for his failures to encompass everything from international copyright conditions to conservative publishing policies to spiteful
editors. When he was provoked, he was at his raging best and
lashed out at everything within range; no one within attacking
distance was immune. He charged the publishers with complicity
in a plot to degrade him, damage his reputation, and frustrate
his success. In response to Paine's request to see the manuscript
of the novel *New York* before agreeing to terms, Fawcett wrote
a letter from Rome severing his relations with Paine:

I would prefer putting my *ms.* over a slow fire to sending it to you
under the conditions you name. I am the author of nearly 40 published novels and I don't think my name a *totally* unknown one either

in America or in England. Your note didn't make me in the least
angry, but I must say that it somewhat amused me. . . .

You could just as well have snubbed me two months ago, if that was
your plan, as to snub me now when I am in Rome. How can you
conceivably suppose that after you have written me this "frankly" I
would send you my *ms?* If I were the obscurist writer in the United
States you could not have assumed toward me a more indifferent
and coolly *de haut en bas* manner. Do you fancy that *for an instant*
I would deal with you on any such terms?

. . . I had hoped the "Combined Press" would strike out into new
paths & forsake the old tedious beaten ruts. The whole situation is
now pitiable and disgusting. International Copyright has been a
shameful failure with us thus far. Sensational and trashy English
tales have been preferred at a larger price to strong and able American work at a comparatively small price. Authors are afraid to speak
out—they are afraid of the Gilders and Aldens. Newspapers will not
speak out, because they desire the advertisements of certain magazines. Meanwhile the petty despotism continues and it is a sorry
fact that no American author today, though he should write another
"Vicar of Wakefield" or another "Scarlet Letter," could gain the least
vogue for it unless it were printed by the "Century" or "Harper's."
It is, I think, certainly 15 years since Mr. Alden ever had an opportunity of reading one of my *mss.,* and it will be 15 more if life
spares me so long. As for Mr. Gilder, I told him my views some time
ago with pronounced clearness.

There does not seem to me the faintest conceivable reason why you
should not have made arrangements with me regarding my new serial,
accepting the word of an old and tried writer that it was of *his* best
works—as it is. But you think otherwise, and so the matter ends.[22]

For Fawcett, however, the matter seldom ended in so simple
a fashion; a personal declaration in a letter was never sufficient
expression. In his war against the critics, he had once issued a
public statement calling for humane courtesy in criticism; and,
in his battle with the publishers, he also expressed his views in
print. In the January, 1896, issue of *Author's Journal,* he charged
the publishers with frustrating the aspirations and success of the
talented writer—he had himself in mind—by printing works of
dubious merit in keeping with their own inferior standards of
taste. It was the *Critic* that had responded to his previous on-
slaught against the reviewers, and it was the *Critic,* once again,
that took him to task for his complaint against the publishers:

It seems to be that the unsuccessful author is the most unreasonable person in the world. He is never willing to lay his unsuccess at the door of fate, but goes directly with it to the door of the publisher and there lays it down. Not only does he lay it there, but he calls the whole world to see how he has been wronged, and who has done him the wrong. . . . Mr. Fawcett has a grievance, and that grievance appears to be that he is not a popular author; and he, like the others, blames the publishers and the editors for this unhappy situation. I can understand an author who has never found a publisher cherishing a mild grudge against that class for their denseness in not recognizing his genius, but I cannot see how a writer who has published several books can hold the publishing fraternity responsible for his failure to secure popularity.

In my opinion, the public and the public alone, is responsible. Mr. Fawcett has been writing novels of all kinds for a number of years, and the public certainly knows him, for the publishers will give the public what it wants—that is what they are in business for. They are not an organized band formed for the sole purpose of squelching the popular author, as so many unpopular authors suppose. I do not like to set up my own commonsense as superior to that of Mr. Fawcett, or any other author with a grievance, but it does seem to me that, if I were so fortunate as to get a book published and so unfortunate as not to have it sell, I should hardly blame the publisher for that misfortune, or think him a curmudgeon, if he preferred to publish the books of an author that the public wanted to read. I might rail at the bad taste of the public, but I do not see how I could have any quarrel with the publisher.[23]

This article of sweetness and light, touched with a tone of restraint, appears to penetrate to the heart of Fawcett's rationalizations; but its extreme oversimplification is misleading on several counts. Commercial considerations *did* frustrate American authorship; popular taste alone did *not* determine literary success or failure; and publishers *were* responsible for the creation of conditions that stifled American literary development. Since there were neither protections nor safeguards of an international copyright agreement, the best and most popular works of English authors were printed in this country at unbelievably low costs; so long as these works were freely acquired, American writings had little chance for publication and small possibility, when published, of competing successfully in the cheap-book market.

Hellmut Lehmann-Haupt in *The Book in America* maintains that, as a result of this situation, vigorous American authorship did not become possible until after the date of the international copyright agreement in 1891.[24]

An additional oversimplification in the *Critic's* retort to Fawcett exists in its oversimplification of Fawcett himself. Fawcett did not wholly "lay his unsuccess at the door . . . of the publisher"; he also held the critics responsible—for the critic molded opinion, and the publisher catered to it.

III *The Public and the Martyr*

Beyond the critics and the publishers, there was still a third antagonistic force that Fawcett deemed culpable in his failure to achieve recognition, success, and reputation. Upon occasion he was prone to look within rather than without; and, at such moments, he held the vitality of his own expression accountable for his failure. It was not his literary inadequacy that he felt alienated the reading public but his expression of radical literary and social views. In fact, he frequently attributed his poor reception to the public's rejection of his thought or to its inability to comprehend his advanced views. He was, he believed, a man ahead of his times, who would have to suffer the common destiny of all men of vision and radical pronouncement.

What Fawcett had in mind when he cast himself in this romantic, Promethean role of antagonist to the Establishment were his uncompromising agnostic point of view; his attacks on the clergy; his contempt for the selfishness and arrogance of the entrenched aristocracy; his justification, if not advocacy, of social revolution; and his self-styled literary heresies. Not one of his expressions on any of these subjects was calculated to endear him to critic, publisher, or public.

Fawcett knew the agnostic to be out of step in a Christian culture; but, because he held agnosticsm to be the highest expression of man's rational thought, he became one of the movement's most outspoken skeptics. In his essay "Agnosticism," he argued that the existence of Christ was by no means a proven fact and that "the ridiculous story that he was born of a virgin is scarcely less to be respected by unbiased judges than the story that he was ever born at all. He is a figure not a whit more actual than Helen of Sparta, Achilles, or Hector," he insisted; "and the entire legend of his crucifixion has no more historic weight than that of the siege of Troy."[25]

The reward for the expression of this unpopular view was disparagement, but Fawcett consoled himself in the belief that a future time would acknowledge the worth of his argument. "What a debt do we owe to the ancestors that freed us from superstition's trammeling tyrannies!" he proclaimed. "A like debt will our successors owe to us in the ages unborn. This realization must content the agnostic."[26] Fawcett often conjured up these future glories to compensate for the attacks leveled against him in his own time. In his poem "To Robert G. Ingersoll" he contemplated an age when science would reign and his own thought would be honored:

> In oblivion our lots will be cast
> When the future hath built firm and fair
>   on the bulk of a petrified past.
> Yet its edifice hardier shall bide for
>   the boons fraught with help that
>   we give—
> For the wrongs that we cope with and
>   slay, for the lies that we crush
>   and outlive![27]

There were other provocative views Fawcett held. As an adversary of an apologetic Christianity, he alienated the clergy: "If the working-girl of New York has any arch foe it is that sad fraud which today is termed Christianity. If today there is any class of men who entirely desert the requirements of their avowed profession it is the class of the clergy."[28] As a foe of an entrenched aristocracy, he did not endear himself to the influential. "The great point with plutocracy and snobbery," he reasoned, "is to perpetuate themselves—to go on producing scions who will uphold for them future generations of selfishness and arrogance. One sees the same sort of procreative tendency in certain of our hardiest and coarsest weeds. Sometimes a gardener comes along with hoe, spade, and a strong uprooting animus. In human life that kind of gardener goes by the ugly name of Revolution."[29]

Fawcett was never unaware of the harmful consequences of his forthrightness. In a letter dated October 18, to "Dear Sir," he wrote: "Shall you care to use this paper, which I have just finished, for $50 (payable on *acceptance,* not *publication*) in your magazine? Though my views on N.Y. Society, as here expressed, are in the strongest way sincere, I have little doubt that they will provoke much discussion and possibly indignation as well."[30]

The literary heresies that Fawcett propounded were less likely to touch off a popular indignation, but they were heresies, nonetheless, and they did irritate the critics. In his insistence upon claiming for poetry the right to a "dark wrong side," he argued that the most revolting passions and loathsome experiences were worthy of poetic expression; and this obsession with the underside of existence ultimately led him into the lower depths of a Realistic fiction that offended the sensibilities of many critics. And those critics who were not angered by his immoral Realism had unlimited opportunity to rage against Fawcett's amoral Naturalistic novels, which were an outgrowth of his Realistic involvement.

IV *The Critical Argument*

Of the three offenders, Fawcett believed the critics to be his greatest detractors. He questioned the acuity of their perceptions and the honesty of their intentions. "I am afraid," he wrote to Hayne, in 1876, "that I shall not be half as well treated by the N.Y. editors, for they are nearly all arrogant and filled with strange prejudices—literary snobs, in fact, of a sort that dear old Thackeray w*d* have drawn superbly."[31] In another letter, written later that year, Fawcett expressed the same attitude:

Narrowness of judgment, unreasoning prejudice and intolerable obstinacy are the order of the day with most of our magazines; or so I have always found. For example, the *Independent* (as you know, perhaps) thinks me a grossly immoral wretch because I wrote *Purple and Fine Linen,* or rather a seraphic, evangelical creature named Wm Hayes Ward so considers me; and I am sure that if I sent him the most attractively devout hymns conceivable he w*d* decline it on suspicion of its being latently prurient. Do you happen to know this pure creature? Jupiterian look; his gait is modest—some ill-natured people might say that he shambled instead of walking, like a slipshod lady. Altogether his style is rather ladylike. One of his fixed tenets of belief is my own irreclaimable immorality. Honestly & candidly—I consider that the unjust and wholly unprejudiced opinion of this most unpleasant person is, after all, a tolerably good specimen of editorial fairness.[32]

Fawcett scorned evaluation resulting from the application of moral standards rather than esthetic ones, but he seldom considered the judgment of any critical opinion to be accurate no matter what its criterion. He constantly braced himself to receive poor notices; he convinced himself, even before the publication of a work, that the critics would condemn it. "Mr. Howells asked me not long ago to let him recommend my serious poems to Osgood," he wrote to Hayne. "I have already begun to copy them, with numberless alterations. It is an endless task. I doubt if the book will be ready for the publisher before next autumn. *How* the critics will pitch into it."[33]

There were undoubtedly very few easy moments before, during, or after publication for Fawcett. He could never quite erase the specter of the critics from his mind; and it, therefore, comes as no surprise to find that he did not confine his comments on the caliber of criticism and the personality of the critic to his private letters only; he also revealed his convictions in print. In an article for *Lippincott's Monthly Magazine,* in 1887, he railed against the futility of criticism and its destructive capacity in the hands of the venomous critic. He argued that, when the same literary work alternately evoked praise, scorn, and pronouncement of mediocrity from three different newspaper reviewers, the reliability of criticism itself was suspect: "These discordances of opinion are not occasional; they occur every day. They are to my mind the great proof of how absurdly needless are all published comments on books in current newspapers."

Fawcett continued to reason that the futility of criticism was manifest in its inability to arrive at absolute pronouncements and that the shortcomings of the critics were evident in their desire to castigate even the most ineffectual writer, whose only trespass lay in his aspiration:

Why rail against these harmless victims of an illusive will-o'-the-wisp? Why call them names, and stamp upon them, and question Jove himself as to the object of their creation? No service to literature is done by giving them sleepless nights and days of torment. Their feeble books are perfectly sure of dying, without denunciation being hurled at them the moment they are born. Nobody will read them, in any case. Pray do not flatter yourself, fiery-eyed critic, with your furious foot still upon one of their gilt-edged offspring, that you have performed the slightest public benefit by your frenzy of condemnation. You have simply succeeded in making a fellow-creature's heart suffer—nothing more.

If this expression seems to be a mild, impersonal one of annoyance with a general critical practice, then what follows is not; for, in the same article, Fawcett bitterly related a personal anecdote, illustrative of the arrogance, egotism, and damning power of the critic:

One evening about eight years ago, just before the appearance of my first book of poems, "Fantasy and Passion," I went to a reception given at the Lotos Club in New York. Among the assembled guests was a certain person whom some optimists have seriously stated to be a poet.[34] He had a position, then, upon some evening paper as its literary critic; I am not quite sure whether or no it was the journal which he at present represents, though I think not. He had been writing with belligerence and not a little clear malignity about certain poems of mine in the *Atlantic Monthly* and elsewhere, and when I received from a mutual acquaintance his request to cross the room and speak with him, I felt considerable surprise. After very little hesitation, however, I refused point-blank; and yet I sent no uncivil message, since the whole affair was one of quite too much indifference to me for that. As I subsequently learned, however, he became excessively angry on hearing of my unwillingness and indeed lost all control of his temper. "I will kill that man!" he exclaimed to my peaceful and astonished emissary, finishing his sentence with a robust oath, and beginning his next sentence with another. "By——, I've killed bigger men than he is, and I'll kill *him!*" This murderous threat bore no allusion to my own life, but rather to that of my first book of poems, "Fantasy and Passion." On the appearance of that book, the gentleman certainly behaved like a critic with a private graveyard for the corpses of those reputations which he had already wrathfully slain.[35]

In affirmative answer to the question in the article's title—"Should Critics Be Gentlemen?"—Fawcett insisted that "most fair and thoughtful criticism is of necessity kindly"; and he concluded his own attack with the gentle reminder that the first law of criti-

cism is "humane courtesy." Though his own emotional nature was
such that he could not restrain himself from attacking others when
the integrity of literature was at stake, he sincerely wished that
critics would concern themselves only with the recognition of an
author's virtues; unfortunately, he had not long to wait before
being made aware of the futility of his desire. James Lane Allen,
writing in the January 15, 1887, issue of the *Critic*, responded to
this plea by calling attention to Fawcett's critical abuse of Edgar
Allan Poe and by questioning Fawcett's own sense of literary
courtesy.

A critical struggle whose outcome is dependent upon which of
the contestants is more humane and which has the higher morality
can have no respectable victor. It is the right battle, but the standards have little to do with the creative work itself. Yet these were
the concerns; and Fawcett, with some justification, continued to
attack the discourtesy and arrogance of the critics and continued
to hold the misdirected function of criticism responsible for his
slight literary reputation.

The quality of much of Fawcett's poetry and prose, especially
his fictional romances, left much to be desired; therefore, despite
his voluminous production, he remained a minor writer; and no
attempt is being made here to suggest otherwise. It is important,
however, to appreciate that the origin of much of the negative response to Fawcett's writings had its roots in the niggling character
of newspaper reviews, in chaotic conservative publishing conditions, and in Fawcett's own espousal of radical and unpopular beliefs. An understanding of these factors, which were influential in
relegating him to literary obscurity, is crucial to assessing his literary worth; to noting his position in the current of American literature; and, ultimately, to acknowledging his contribution to the
development of Realism and Naturalism in American literature.

CHAPTER 2

Critical Reception

FAWCETT'S scathing condemnation of literary critics alienated
quite a few of these influential men and undoubtedly predis-
posed many of them to react unfavorably to his work. In all fairness to the newspaper and periodical reviewers, however, it must
be said that their criticisms of his Romances were, in the main,
perceptive and valid. Some of the notices were, to be sure, favorable; but the predominant critical response to his "romances" was
sufficiently negative to deny Fawcett the gratification of literary
distinction. The reviews themselves are of considerable value, not
only because they established Fawcett's reputation in his own time,
but because they also illuminated the scope and substance of his
work and defined the areas of his artistic limitations in the writing
of romance—his contrived plot structures, his insubstantial thematic
concerns, his surface characterizations, and his pretentious style.[1]

I *Plot*

The obvious melodrama and theatrics of a Fawcett Romance provided reviewers with an opportunity to utilize a synoptic technique
in conveying their estimate of one of his novels. That is, they merely
presented a plot synopsis that, in its faithful adherence to the details of the novel's movements, carried with it an implicit judgment
of the work. The *Critic* reviewer of *Miriam Balestier*, for example,
reacted against the heavy-handed manipulation of the novel's plot,
the one-dimensional nature of the conflict between the innocent
and the wicked characters, and the fortuitous melodramatic victory
for the forces of good.[2] His synopsis of plot said all of these things
for him:

Miriam Balestier lived in dreary rooms in Bleeker Street. Her mother
drank; her sister was a trial. She had a brother who had written an

opera. Miriam wanted to sing the leading part, if she could get any one to bring the opera out. She took it to a manager, vulgar but human, who refused the thing. Paula, an acquaintance of Miriam's, who went with her, was more vulgar than the manager, but she was more successful than Miriam, for she was engaged to sing in a new operetta. San Francisco was the spot chosen for the production of the musical gem. It was to be brought out by a man who loved Miriam. Paula was jealous of Miriam, but she concealed her jealousy and called her "my dear." Could any deception be cleverer? When Miriam returned from her unsuccessful interview with the vulgar manager, she found her mother drunk, her sister just horrid;. and to round out a state of affairs, her brother struck her because the manager had refused his opera. Miriam therefore went to California with Paula, the man who loved her (erst Paula's lover), and the troupe. One night *en route* Paula induced Miriam to go out on the platform. It was the day before vestibule trains, and Paula, like Mrs. Johnny Sands in the song, was intent upon pushing Miriam off; when—*Ecce deus ex machinâ!*—there was a collision. Paula was killed; Miriam was not.[3]

At times, it was difficult for a critic to distinguish between the melodramatic nature of one of Fawcett's plots and the disjointed movements within the action of the plot. They were closely related; and, all too often, the chance happening, such as Paula's death, erased a villain and permitted virtue to triumph. Thus, any comment upon plot usually revealed an insight into the melodrama of forces *and* the chaos of structure.

Not all reviews took the form of plot synopses, and not all reviewers concerned themselves with the melodramatics of plot. There were some who were capable of disentangling the structure of the plot from its melodramatic nature and passing comment upon the former only. The reviewer for the *Nation* called attention to the haphazard construction of *The Adventures of a Widow* and, in fact, suggested that it was the lack of total unity in Fawcett's works that militated against the fulfillment of his potential. "We sometimes think no one comes so near to great work as Mr. Fawcett," he ventured. "In some conceptions of character, in some detached scenes, he almost attains it, but in a moment he falls so far below it that we wonder at our own faith in him. . . . The poorer chapters . . . are thrown by some failure of perspective into altogether undue prominence. . . . The failure is in the selection of incidents by which the action is carried on."[4]

II *Theme*

Other critics, not concerned with the idiosyncrasies of plot structure, expressed their dissatisfaction with the superficiality of
Fawcett's themes. The reviewer for the *Critic* characterized *A
Demoralizing Marriage* as "shoddy, salacious, sickening," yet he
admitted that he would have welcomed the novel if only "he [Faw-
cett] brought us somewhat nearer to truth by these pictures of de-
moralized humanity."[5] The reviewer's complaint was with the
dreariness of a narrative without purpose, but one suspects that his
judgment was excited by his moral reaction against the Realistic
aspects of the novel, rather than by his esthetic response to the
novel's lack of thematic substance.

This lack of depth in Fawcett's novels—whether of theme or of
character—drew frequent notice. The reviewer of *Social Silhouettes*
in the *Athenaeum* remarked that "Mr. Fawcett is not incisive
enough; in most of his sketches he does not go deeper than the
mere froth of society";[6] and the reviewer for the *Dial* of *The House
at High Bridge* commented upon the same superficiality. He noted
that the main plot had been taken bodily from an English novel,
The Giant's Robe, by a Mr. Guthrie. "The trouble with this plot,"
he maintained, "is that it was not worth taking at all—by Mr.
Fawcett. A great analyst, one knowing profoundly the human heart,
a Balzac, in short, might make an effective central figure of the
unread novelist who becomes famous upon the publication of another man's work as his own, but the present writer is so far from
being a Balzac that he cannot make such a figure even interesting."[7]

III *Characterization*

Fawcett's frequent inability to invest a plot with profound meaning suggests his failure to penetrate to the complexity of movement
and to illuminate the dilemma of conflicting forces. This failing,
however, was not the only weakness the critics observed. When
the reviewer for the *Dial* remarked that Fawcett was unable to
make his leading figure even mildly interesting, he touched upon
a faultiness in characterization that other critics also noted. Fawcett
designed his protagonists to be men and women of heroic propor-
tions. He endowed them with sound minds and sound bodies; he
graced them with unassailable characters, magnetic personalities,
and penetrating wits. Occasionally, he imposed a weakness upon

one, a tragic flaw; but the chink in the armor was of such insubstantial stuff that it never truly threatened an ultimate victory.

The attributes of these heroes were grand, but there was only the word of the omniscient author to testify to their existence. Fawcett asserted their qualities into being; he seldom established them through action, thought, or dialogue. The *New York Times* review of *A Mild Barbarian* offered comment upon the result of this sort of characterization: "Mr. Fawcett, perhaps, started out to draw the picture of a perfect man, morally, physically, intellectually perfect, and entirely uncontaminated by the evil influences of modern society. He has, however, simply pictured a rather amiable, but frequently inconsistent boor, without much blood in his veins. The task Mr. Fawcett set for himself evidently required more patient toil and more thought than he has expended on its execution."[8]

Two other reviews from the *New York Times* concurred with this judgment; their expression was so similar that it is more than likely they were written by the same man. In 1880, the reviewer of *A Hopeless Case* observed that:

Oscar Schuyler is the cynical gentleman of the book, for "in a certain way he was feared; people often cultivated him to gain his good-will; the celebrity of his biting tongue silenced would-be adversaries, it was like the famed spear of Lancelot, at whose first blow, however slight, tough warriors went down." The cynic in the story under review is not very mordant. He rather recalls from Mr. Fawcett's description of him what Saint Beuve tells about Mlle. Scudéry. This lady had a charming way of complimenting herself, and in her dialogues, when anybody said anything which she thought was fairly good, the reply she placed in the mouth of the person who answered was: *"Tout ce que vous dites est bien dit,"* or *"Tout cela est merveilleusement trouvé."* [9]

The 1883 *Times* review of *An Ambitious Woman* echoed the observation and the words:

The dialogue, the most difficult task of the novelist, shows rather the eccentricities of the personages than their mental differences. Mrs. Diggs says to Claire, "I never saw you so *spirituelle,* Claire. You have said at least 18 delicious things." Readers are never inclined to accept such declarations of brilliancy on the sole authority of the author. Saint Beuve laughs at Mlle. de Scudéry for this method of complimenting her own characters. The platitude of one speaker was followed in the dialogue by another person's saying, "*Tout ce que vous dites est bien dit,*" or "*Tout cela est merveilleusement trouve.*"[10]

It is difficult to conceive of anything other than a common origin for these two reviews; but whether or not the views were separately formulated is of no consequence. Such responsible and perceptive criticism reveals a limitation of Fawcett's art, even though Fawcett himself would have taken exception, since he considered strength of characterization to be one of the outstanding achievements of his fiction. "I am very glad that you think Archie well-drawn," he wrote to Hayne with reference to *Ellen Story,* "and that you see so keenly just what I meant Ellen to be. Your own words express perfectly the ideal of her that I myself had formed. It is a great literary achievement to have drawn one really noble & true woman in a large Titianesque way."[11] In 1879, three years later, in another letter to Hayne, Fawcett evidenced the same pride of accomplishment in his delineation of character: "Saltus tells me that you like 'Rutherford.' That is welcome news. I worked terribly hard over the portraitures in that book; I tried to do it altogether in the grand manner, & make artistic repose its chief excellence."[12]

Fawcett's intentions, however, did not constitute accomplishment in the opinion of the critics. In another comment on *A Hopeless Case,* this time from the *Atlantic Monthly,* the reviewer remarked upon the one-dimensional aspect of characterization: "He [Fawcett] has seen the woman beneath the fashionable figure, and has presented her to our respect. Now given this sincerity and real humanness, we contend that Agnes Wolverton, with all her fine sentiments, failed clearly to discern it [the shallowness of aristocratic manners], and our complaint is that Mr. Fawcett has tried his hand at depicting a girl of a higher plane, and has left out the true woman." This weakness in the novel's characterization was a damning defect; for it was the reviewer's final opinion that, were it not for this one flaw, "as a portraiture of New York society, it seems . . . exceptionally clever."[13]

IV *Prose Style*

The reviewers directed much of their attention to what they considered to be Fawcett's inept handling of characterization, his contrived plots, and his insubstantial themes; they also touched upon other aspects of his writing. In fact, references to Fawcett's turgid prose and to his hyperbolic expression permeated almost every commentary. Of *A Man's Will*, the *Nation* criticized a style "cursed with adverbs, pompous and viscid."[14] The *New York Times's* observation was of a kind: "The author of 'Tinkling Cymbals' is always overfond of presenting the toilets of his heroines. Women wear zones of silver, or assort their complexions to their gowns, and bonnets are so minutely described that an intelligent milliner of Division Street might buy Mr. Fawcett's novels and follow his text for patterns."[15] And, with reference to the same novel, the *Nation* reviewer had much the same reaction: "Mr. Fawcett cannot afford to neglect his English. 'Flinchless,' and 'wafture,' and 'the indulgent period' would have a doubtful sound anywhere, and all the more in a style that turns easily to large phrases."[16]

The *Athenaeum*, in the same vein, noted that Fawcett's studies in *Social Silhouettes* were, as a rule, "too long, and details which are not essential are over-elaborated."[17] The *New York Times* maintained of *Rutherford* that "it is Mr. Fawcett's chiefest fault that he is immensely elaborate."[18] Of course, Fawcett dissented from these opinions; in a letter to Hayne, he contended that *Rutherford* was "poetic, elegant, sonorously rhetorical and generally classical in style."[19] But the collective sound of critical judgment diminished the resonance of Fawcett's voice. The reviewer for the *Catholic World* pronounced that Fawcett, in *A New York Family*, "has never, to our knowledge, written so seriously and so well," but he also observed that though Fawcett's style was "far more unaffected than usual," he had "not yet shaken off his fondness for employing common words in remote and unaccustomed senses. Thus he says of Everard, on one occasion, that his 'lovely personality *disarrayed*' another man, and that without the slightest intention on his own part to dismay the reader's imagination."[20]

The *Atlantic Monthly* contributed its opinion to the body of comment. The reviewer of *An Ambitious Woman* noted that Fawcett "everywhere shows a taste for gaudy and florid expression . . . elaborating trifles of statement in overloaded and forced phrases."[21] And the *New York Times* summarized prevailing critical opinion in its lengthy review of the same novel:

Over-elaborateness is Mr. Fawcett's peculiarity. In the treatment of that special subject he so delights in, New York society, he incumbers his stage with properties. The toilets of women, the dress of the men, the upholstery of drawing-rooms, the garniture of the supper table, are described with infinite pains. Claire Hollister, the heroine, puts on a dress of white velvet, "whose trailing heaviness blent with purple lengths of the same lustreless and sculpturesque fabric." In her hair she wore "aigrettes of sapphires and amethysts shaped like pansies, and while her sleeves were cut short to show either arm from wrist to elbow and permit of bracelets that were circles of jewels wrought in semblance of the same flower and with the same blue or lilac gems, her bust and throat were clad in one cloud of rare filmy lace, from which her delicate head rose with a stately and aerial grace." . . .

One mannerism of Mr. Fawcett's method of writing is the over-use of qualifying adjectives. The idiosyncrasies of a character may adopt this style, and Mrs. Diggs may call Jane Van Corlear, "a dear consistent, inoffensive, companionable goose," or declare her to be "tallowy, obese, complaisant"—but Mr. Fawcett in his picturing of objects, animate or inanimate, constantly piles on the descriptive. There is too much that is finicky in Mr. Fawcett's metaphors. . . . The element of spontaneity of expression seems to be often wanting . . . . His work smells too much of the oil.[22]

CHAPTER *3*

Fawcett and Romance

THE reviewers' adverse critical opinions of Fawcett's novels were well founded, and their preconceptions were substantially correct. It would be misleading, however, to assume that their remarks were equally pertinent to all of Fawcett's novels. The weaknesses they noted of plot, theme, characterization, design, and execution are less evident in Fawcett's Realistic and Naturalistic novels; they are, in the main, the debilitating trademark of his romantic novels and, for that matter, of most popular romances written during the last quarter of the nineteenth century.

Romances are fanciful rather than Realistic works of prose fiction, and thus their scope extends across an infinite plain of imaginative experience, constantly revealing an affinity for the exotic and adventurous rather than for the pedestrian and the probable. It would, therefore, seem that there would be little likelihood of two romances resembling each other in matters of substance; and yet it is most difficult to distinguish one late nineteenth-century romance from another, for most were spun from the same time-worn yarn and were laid out against the same time-honored pattern. The thing of wonder in these Romances is not to be found in the unique features of any one of them but in the similarity of all, when created by so many different hands. Fawcett's *Divided Lives* (1888)[1] is a remarkable model of this popular genre; it is replete with melodramatic situation, exaggerated emotions, contrived incidents, pure passions, villainous deeds, stock characters, and noble love.

The novel begins with the triangle of love. Hubert Throckmorton, poet and author of the anonymously printed romance, *Glenalvan,* is in love with Angela Laight. Mrs. Prescott Averill, who is in love with Throckmorton, commits the first treachery of the affair by convincing Angela of Throckmorton's unfaithfulness to her. Angela, believing the slander, marries Bleakly Voght, an old, but ardent, millionaire. Mrs. Averill's confession of the slander and her death complete the first half of the action.

In the second half of the novel, Throckmorton and Angela meet, confess their love for each other, but promise to respect her marriage vows; Angela returns to her loveless marriage and Throckmorton to his poetry. In a sudden turn of events, however, Voght is killed by Julius Bradbourne Heath, brother of Jane Heath, a woman Voght had seduced and who had borne his illegitimate child. Throckmorton is at first accused of the murder, but he is cleared, and the way opens for Angela and Throckmorton to consummate their love. The novel meets its romantic requirements, yet Fawcett must have held it to be of some integrity and worth; for he dedicated it "To my friend, George Parsons Lathrop, poet and novelist, in the hope that many prosperous days may be apportioned to a writer whom the letters of his land so ill can spare."

Fawcett wrote three such novels in 1888, but none was so devoid of literary worth and significant matter as *Divided Lives. Miriam Balestier*,[2] for example, has its share of love, treachery, near murder, accident, intrigue, and happy ending, with the reunion of the parted lovers; but it also offers a deterministic view of life that rescues it from its romantic trappings. Miriam's early movements in the novel are all reactions to her squalid and brutal surroundings. Her family lives in a dingy apartment in New York's Lower East Side; her mother is an alcoholic, her sister is vulgar, and her brother is an opportunist who would have her sell her honor for his gain. Miriam tries to transcend her environment, but her efforts are futile and seem doomed to failure (environment holds sway) until a chance accident places her in the bosom of a rural family, where she is treated with a love and affection she had never known before. The new set of surroundings reshapes her character and destiny; the change is for the better, which satisfies the requirements of the Romance, but of far greater importance to the deterministic implications of the novel is the fact that change has taken place at all. Environment, be it for good or ill, is the ultimate determiner of all behavior; chance provides the only means to alter one's destiny.

Olivia Delaphaine,[3] Fawcett's third 1888 romance, is almost a carbon copy of *Divided Lives*. Olivia, like Angela Laight, is tricked into marriage with an extremely wealthy older man, Spencer Delaplaine. The novel documents her noble sufferings until Delaplaine dies and Olivia is free to marry Jasper Massereene, the handsome lover, who had been faithfully waiting at her side. Within the framework of so slight a structure, Fawcett injected a number of rather interesting reflections and portraits. There are allusions to English and American cultural differences, a concern that occupied a place of central importance in his more serious fiction. Here, the references are fleeting, but they are pertinent to the development of plot, for both Massereene and Olivia were reared in Europe, and their shared insights into the decadence of New York societal manner establish the foundation of their love.

Fawcett also managed to inject into the novel an interesting portrait of Olivia's aunt, Mrs. Satterthwaite, and her wealthy friends. Society life is an empty, meaningless, but maddening whirl of soirees, at homes, dinners, balls, and promenades. The whirl is the epitome of vacuity, yet Lucy Satterthwaite, Olivia's cousin, is sacrificed to the wastefulness of it all. She is a young girl of slight energy who attempts to keep pace with her elders; she fails, and, in what is undoubtedly the most taut and provocative line of the novel, Fawcett records that she "watched her elders and thought it was a capital idea to do as they were doing. She did and it killed her."[4]

Fawcett slackened his pace in 1890 and dropped his production to only two romantic novels, neither of which had much to recommend it, although one, *How a Husband Forgave*,[5] purported to be of some depth. Wallace Waldo, the husband of the title, falls in love with and marries Cecilia Brinckerhoff. After the marriage, Cecilia becomes friendly with Wallace's friend, Paul Godfrey, a novelist, and the two spend a great deal of time with each other as Wallace is always busy at the office. It turns out that Wallace is not really at the office; he is in the company of Charlotte Parselle, an old flame, and Kitty Claye, a woman of notoriety. Cecilia finds out and attacks Wallace, who feels not only contrite but also misunderstood—a woman should not be so possessive, he argues, and she should understand a man's needs. Needless to say, Cecilia does not. Wallace goes abroad with Kitty, and Cecilia stays home and has an affair with Godfrey, which she justifies to herself on the grounds of her honest passion and her right to equal privileges.

When Wallace returns, Charlotte Parselle informs him of his wife's behavior in his absence, and Cecilia and Wallace then have their confrontation. With calm dignity and apparent pride, she admits to her indiscretions. He leaves, spends a sleepless night, finds it in himself to forgive her, has a secret talk with Godfrey, and then returns to her in the morning. The reunited husband and wife go abroad for a number of years, return with a son, live a quiet life, devoted to one another, and have very little to do with social affairs. Paul Godfrey becomes a noted man of letters but lives as a hermit on Lexington Avenue.

Fawcett's serious intent in the novel centers upon the defiance of Cecilia. She is not an innocent ingenue, duped into an affair with a treacherous male; she is aware of her actions, quite enamored of Godfrey, and, when found out, she does not beg forgiveness but asserts her rights. The equal-rights movement for women had a compelling fascination for Fawcett; he created a gallery of independent women in his novels: Rosalind Maturin in *A Demoralizing Marriage*, Claire Twining in *An Ambitious Woman*, Agnes Wolverton in *A Hopeless Case*, and Elizabeth Romilly in *Tinkling Cymbals*, to name but a few. Cecilia Brinckerhoff belongs to this same sisterhood, although in spirit only; for the situation she finds herself in is so obviously contrived and conventional that it detracts from the vitality of her assertion of equality.

A Daughter of Silence,[6] also written in 1890, begins with a dedication to William Cutterson Wood of Durham, England, "with regrets that I have no gift more suited to his sunny mind and winsome nature than this tale, so sombre in coloring, of destiny's most bitter defeats." The novel is somber, a romance of dark love; but it is difficult to determine exactly what Fawcett had in mind when he conceived it as a tale of "destiny's most bitter defeats." The daughter of silence is Brenda Monk, a beautiful but passive woman, who becomes engaged to Guy Arbuthnot. During the period of their engagement, Brenda's father is murdered by Ralph Allaire, an erstwhile friend of Brenda's. Brenda visits Allaire in his prison cell and hands him the knife he had used to kill her father; Allaire stabs himself and dies. Brenda comes out of his cell, confesses to Arbuthnot that she had been Allaire's mistress for three years, and then kills herself with the same knife. The novel moves at a swift pace, and enough information is held back along the way to create an atmosphere of suspense; but, despite Fawcett's enigmatic comment in the dedication, the novel offers little insight into human destiny or, for that matter, into anything at all.

Women Must Weep (1891)[7] is an ambitious novel inasmuch as Fawcett tried to interweave three love affairs into one coherent pattern to illuminate the servility of women in marriage. However, the novel departs from his usual format in that the characters are not the elevated figures of romance, but the middle-class sufferers of Realism. Nonetheless, the intrigues of the novel, the exaggerated emotions, and the noble sufferings place the work in closer harmony with Fawcett's romantic rather than Realistic tone.

The three daughters of Isaac Trask, an apothecary, are left to fend for themselves after his death. Eunice, the eldest, marries Austin Legree, a clerk in Trask's store, who turns out to be a savage, domineering, bully of a husband. Dora, the middle daughter, marries Harvey Kinnicutt, a promising young newspaperman, who is weak, has a fatal attraction for women, and often strays. Annette, the youngest, marries Gordon Ammidown, an extremely wealthy young man, who, unknown to her, is an alcoholic. The unhappiness of all three marriages bears out Aunt Liza Heffernan's early presentiments about marriage: " 'What I mean's this, Andy,' she continued: 'Us women, as regards marriage, are the under-dogs in the fight. I've thought it all over; I know I'm right about it, too. There's three things that pester and torment us when we get to be wives. Most of the men—I won't say all of 'em, but most—either don't stay true, or else they drink more or less bad, or else they're regular devils in their own homes. Devils, I mean,' she added, 'that behave like angels outside.' "[8]

Eunice throws her husband out because he strikes her; Dora does the same to Harvey because he cannot put an end to his affairs with other women; and Annette is deprived of her husband when he is killed in a drunken barroom brawl. Dora finally relents and takes Harvey back, not because he has changed, but because she feels a woman must accept the shortcomings of a man if she is to be a wife. In conclusion, Annette argues that, had she been Eunice, she would not have forced a separation with her husband; and Eunice insists that she was right in refusing to live with a weak man who had abused her. The virtue of conciliation in marriage is then discussed by the three sisters, but the issue is not resolved. Though Fawcett again touched upon the question of the emerging independence of women and the insecurities of their existence in a double-standard culture, the novel merely suggests, after it examines the institution of marriage, that men have the better of it and that "Women Must Weep."

Loaded Dice,[9] Fawcett's second romance of 1891, is pure froth, adventure, and escapism, without the burden of a single redeeming social idea. The international adventuress of the novel, Camilla Blandthwaite, ex-mistress of Abbott Ogilvie, plans to captivate and ensnare Philip Dwinelle, noted young American author and friend of Ogilvie. Monsieur Duquesne, a continental lover and man of mystery, who is hopelessly in love with Camilla, tells Dwinelle of her sordid past. Dwinelle, horrified at Camilla's lack of propriety, leaves her, and she, in turn, punishes Duquesne for his treachery by refusing ever to see him again. Duquesne is frantic without Camilla's love. He is arrested for theft; but, before he is taken to jail, he manages to kill Camilla and then himself. At the end of the novel, Ogilvie pulls the one loose strand into place by marrying Lady Ethel Trefusis, who had been a forced companion to Camilia.

In *The Adopted Daughter*,[10] published in 1892, Fawcett returned to romance with a purpose. Marie Rouncevalle, living in Europe with her expatriate American mother, is really the daughter of Hugh Costello, a corrupt New York politician. The Costellos had given their daughter to the Rouncevalles when she was an infant, and they now want her back. Marie, her mother, and her fiancé, Eustace Amory, an honest American politician, all return to America to thrash things out with the Costellos. Under Marie's influence, her father undergoes transformation from a corrupt to a reform politico; and the Rouncevalles, mother and daughter, plus Amory, decide to remain in America rather than return to Europe.

The Adopted Daughter, like *Olivia Delaplaine*, offers a smattering of insight into the affairs of the international novel. The blend of Marie's European concept of leadership, Amory's American dedication to idealism and principle, and Costello's American mien of strength and forcefulness, offers promise of a new era in man's social development. In Fawcett's international novels, he usually pointed to the distinct attributes of the New and Old World; and he presented an ideal society emanating from a synthesis of virtues —in this instance, a tempering of American crudeness with European manner and an enlivening of European stodginess with American vitality.

Her Fair Fame (1894)[11] lays claim to being the poorest novel Fawcett ever wrote. A dull affair, it completely lacks the suspense, excitement, or sophistication of his other romances. The novel presents itself seriously, and that is, perhaps, its chief fault; the matter is too slight, too theatrical, and too vapid to be seriously digested.

Ogden Hamilton is Phyllis Lorremore's guardian. He is secretly in
love with her, but she marries his protégé, Foulke Bradford, a
struggling young artist. After six wonderful years of poverty and
starvation, Bradford becomes ill and death beckons. Hamilton re-
appears in time to promise Bradford the medical aid he needs if
Phyllis will return to him as his ward. Phyllis, motivated by her
love for her husband, agrees to live with the old man once more.
Two years later, Bradford and Phyllis find each other again—he
has since become a successful painter—and Hamilton, suffering the
remorse of his dastardly attempts to separate the two young lovers,
kills himself.

In *A Romance of Old New York* (1897),[12] Fawcett worked in
his lighter mood. The plot of the novel has little more to recommend itself than that of *Her Fair Fame,* but Fawcett managed to
escape its dreariness by coloring his events with a touch of bright-
ness and with a dash of the grand action. The setting of the novel
is in a past, statelier era of New York's history; Aaron Burr, whom
Fawcett characterizes as a misunderstood patriot, a fearless leader,
and a romantic lover, takes his place as one of the characters in the
drama, thereby investing it with a background of glamor and a
sense of historicity.

The frame of the novel follows the affairs of two sisters, Charlotte
and Pamela Verplanck, and their respective gentlemen callers, Mark
Frankland and Gerald Suydam. Pamela, the spoiled and spiteful
sister, insists she is in love with Charlotte's beau, Mark Frankland;
and the Verplanck family insists, therefore, that Frankland marry
Pamela. The couples, following the advice of Aaron Burr, who is
all-knowing in these affairs of the heart, straighten themselves out
and depart for happiness-ever-after land.

Fawcett wrote three other non-Realistic novels—*Solarion*
(1889),[13] *The New Nero* (1893),[14] and *The Ghost of Guy Thyrle*
(1896)[15]—that were not of a piece with the standard fare of his romances. They were journeys into the mind, excursions into fantasy;
each one is fresh, inventive, and certainly experimental for its time.

Solarion is the story of Kenneth Rodney Stafford, an American
from Vermont with a Faustian thirst for knowledge. While journey-
ing in Strasbourg, Stafford meets Herr Klotz, a scientist, who has
but a short time to live. Klotz makes Stafford promise that, upon
his death, he will destroy the results of his life-long research; but
Stafford violates this deathbed wish and returns to Vermont with

the fruits of Klotz's research, where his experiments with electrical current result in the birth of Solarion, a dog he endows with the power of speech. Solarion has the power to communicate; but, even more astounding, he has the mind and learning ability of a marked genius. Stafford lives a rare, idyllic life with Solarion until the dog asserts his independence by announcing that he prefers to live with Stafford's ex-fiancée. Stafford, sorely upset by Solarion's infidelity, kills the dog, but not before Solarion destroys half his face.

The sheer fantasy of the novel is intriguing; yet the undertones are even more so, as Fawcett, anticipating the twentieth century, runs a disturbing Freudian thread throughout the entire work. When Stafford was a little boy, he was most precious and beautiful. He had a decidedly girlish look, and his mother fostered his effeminate appearance by keeping him in long, heavy, golden curls until his friends nearly drove him to hysteria by calling him "girl-boy" and "missy." When his mother died, he was stricken with grief, and it was then he began his quest for knowledge that resulted in the creation of Solarion.

Solarion is the embodiment of Stafford as a little boy, but he is more than a re-creation of self for the young man: he also offers Stafford the comfort and serenity of a relationship he had not known since his mother died. On many of their evenings at home, Stafford buries his head in Solarion's "soft, silky curls" and vows his affection to the faithful and loving dog. When his sweetheart decides to marry another man, Stafford does not kill her; but, when Solarion announces his intention of rejecting him, Stafford becomes maddened and, in what can only be interpreted as a lover's quarrel, shoots the dog. The fact that Solarion never speaks to a human being other than Stafford underscores Fawcett's evident intent of presenting a bizarre journey through the oedipal passage of Stafford's mind.

The New Nero pales alongside the eerie doings of *Solarion*; it is not nearly so fantastic a work, but it is, nonetheless, a decided fantasy. Fanshawe, the protagonist of the novel, visits his uncle, Dr. Theobald, a resident physician at a New England mental hospital. When his uncle leaves him alone for a period of time, Fanshawe is accosted by an inmate who claims to be Harold Mountstuart, the man who had murdered seven of his family to gain an inheritance. His problem, he explains to Fanshawe, is that he wishes to be punished; but he so cleverly had planned and executed the murders that no one will believe his guilt. He leaves Fanshawe a manuscript to read, the confession of the seven murders. Fanshawe reads the manuscript, which constitutes the major portion of the novel; and he is convinced that Mountstuart is indeed guilty and indeed sane. Dr. Theobald then returns and explains to his nephew that the man he met was not Mountstuart—in fact, there is no such person as Mountstuart—but Fleming Lancewood, a brilliant and mad novelist.

Fawcett's interest in the relationship between fiction and reality is at the core of the novel, and the fantasy quality of the work projects outward from this concern. Lancewood's fabrication is so vivid and imaginative that Fanshawe takes it for reality, whereas his uncle's rationality is so logically fashioned that he is reluctant to accept it as truth. He prefers his truth, or reality, to possess the excitement and implausibility of fiction. In short, the creation of Realism in fiction is not necessarily bound to the novelist's adherence to the truth of detail; the creation, and the attraction, of literary Realism may well lie in the artist's fancy and in his execution rather than in his *donnée*. Thus, despite Dr. Theobald's assertion of truth at the conclusion of the novel, one is left wondering whether or not there is a Harold Mountstuart; for the narrative seems too compelling to be a mere fictional escapade into fancy.

In *The Ghost of Guy Thyrle*, Fawcett once again concerned himself with an aberration of the mind. This time, however, he did not journey within to probe the recesses of mental disorder; he externalized the process by projecting one half of the split personality into a separate and independent existence. Guy Thyrle's experiments with Onarline, a drug of his own manufacture, become the springboard for his spiritual adventures. Under the influence of Onarline, he is able to propel his spiritual self out of his physical self and into the astral sphere. While Thyrle is in his spiritual nirvana, his body remains an inert corporeal mass, waiting upon the reentry of the spirit for its revivification. Thyrle shares the secret of Onarline with his friend, Vincent Ardilange; but Ardilange proves to be treacherous; and, the next time Thyrle makes his journey, Ardilange has his body cremated. Thyrle's spirit, or ghost, must thus wander through the universe for eternity.

The description of Thyrle's experiences are narcotic projections of the overactive imagination. His transcendent spirit, once freed from its bone-house, mean-house, finds its freedom in the aery

universe of infinity. Like all narcotic visions into the infinite, however, the escapade is limited by the finite duration of the dream,
which, in the odyssey of Guy Thyrle, is extended into the frightening realm of nightmare. By disintegrating his being, he trades the
secure confinement of his body for the awesome confinement of the
universe; and there is no return from the corridors of one's own
imagination.

CHAPTER *4*

Realism, Morality, The Critics, and Fawcett

THE criticism of Fawcett's romantic novels swayed from the
occasional comment of praise to the more frequent note of
disapproval; and, in so doing, it established judgment and revealed
the subject matter of Fawcett's works; but these ends were not vital
to the main consideration of late nineteenth-century critical thought.
The significant critical debate at this time had little to do with the
complexity of literary characterization, the soundness of plot construction, the profundity of theme, and the grace of diction. Such
concerns were peripheral to the argument over the merits of the
romantic, the Realistic, and the Naturalistic work.[1] This new controversy was widespread; it affected almost all of the periodical
criticism of the time; and it shaped a substantial part of the comment on Fawcett's novels. In order to appreciate fully the role
Fawcett played in this movement, it is essential to probe the intensity of the critical argument and to understand its nature.

I *The Critical Debate*

A writer in the *Forum* in 1888 characterized the literary clash
as "The New Battle of the Books." "For a long time," he maintained,
"a wordy war has raged in the magazines and the newspapers between so-called realists and romanticists. In *Harper's Monthly* Mr.
Howells has been asserting the importance of novels that keep close
to the fact of life; and the critics and criticasters have daily attacked
his teaching and practice as materialistic and debasing . . . the
ground is strewn with dead and dying reputations." [2]

Although both sides in the struggle assumed a confident manner,
there were occasional notes of despair. Nancy Banks, reacting to
the publication of Frank Norris's *McTeague* (1899), lamented that
"the passing of morbid realism has never been quite so complete
as the healthy-minded hoped it would be, when it was swept out

of sight five or six years ago by the sudden on-rush of ideality and romance which arose like a fresh, sweet wind to clear the literary atmosphere. In this resistless new movement toward light and hope and peace, these black books were cast aside and forgotten, and there was fair hope for a time that the celebration of the painful and unclean had passed from fiction forever."[3]

It is not possible to determine whether Miss Banks formulated her bias in accordance with her moral convictions or her esthetic judgments, for both factors shaped the response to the Realistic work. Reflections of reality offended the moral sensibilities of many critics who believed that the narration of base actions impaired artistic expression. They argued that "this country is flooded with a nasty literature that is not only crude, but as low in tone as it is atrocious in taste."[4] Amelia Barr's comment on the late nineteenth-century heroine, in the *North American Review*, typified the unfortunate synthesis of literary and moral judgment so common in periodical criticism of the time:

The one thing to be regretted in many of the lighter novels of the day is their kind of heroine. She is not a nice girl. She talks too much, and talks in a slangy, jerky way, that is odiously vulgar. She is frank, too frank, on every subject and occasion. She is contemptuous of authority, even of parental authority, and behaves in a high-handed way about her love affairs. She is, alas! something of a Freethinker. She rides a bicycle and plays tennis, and rows a boat. She laughs loudly, and dresses in manly fashion, and acts altogether in accord with an epoch that travels its sixty miles an hour. She is very smart and clever, but in her better moments she makes us sigh for the girls who thought their parents infallible and who were reverent church-women—the girls who were so shrinkingly modest, and yet so brave in great emergencies—the girls who were so fully accomplished and so beautiful, and who yet had no higher ambition than to be the dearly loved wife of a noble-hearted man and the good house-mother of happy children. Perhaps fifty years after this, the world will look back to this picturesque, lovable creature, and give her a glorious resurrection.[5]

Even the critical writings of William Dean Howells were not entirely free from this confusion of moral and esthetic values. Without equivocation, Howells argued that the Realist can hold *nothing* to be insignificant in life, if he is to raise truth from its obscure mirings. "All tells for destiny and character; nothing that God has made is contemptible," he declared. "He [the Realist] cannot look upon human life and declare this thing or that thing unworthy of notice, any more than the scientist can declare a fact of the material world beneath the dignity of his inquiry." And yet, in the same essay, Howells, who defended the writings of Henrik Ibsen and Émile Zola, compromised the force of his esthetic assertion by suggesting in moral tones that the novel should concern itself only with sentiment that "could be openly spoken of before the tenderest society bud at dinner."[6]

On the one side of the controversy were those who believed the function of literature to be the evocation of truth through the reflection of the mundane; on the other side were those who discerned literary merit only in the emergence of a transcendent beauty removed from the rigors of everyday existence. These were the separate literary faiths, but considerations of morality entered in on both sides and influenced judgment. Fawcett's Realistic works were at the heart of this argument, and they provoked comments that reflected this position.

II *The Response to Realism*

The *New York Times* reviewer of *Tinkling Cymbals,* considering a reflection of the actual to be a standard in the determination of literary merit, judged that the novel had "a very good story, and, in a certain way, reflects the manners of a great many snobbish people."[7] The observation that the novel accurately reflected certain manners was not unrelated to the reviewer's judgment itself, for the substance of the critique suggested that the work was good precisely because it mirrored existing manners. Another *New York Times* review of a Fawcett novel, printed fifteen years later, in 1898, presented the same criterion for evaluation; the critic praised *New York* because it was "much like the real world of Gotham." He hailed the novel as

a notable addition to the hundred and one stories inspired by Gotham and its life. . . . Mr. Fawcett . . . pictures the slums of Water Street and its environs, the regions of Cherry Hill and its denizens, the missions and that form of charity that is too purposeful and too important to be given its cant name of "slumming." Weaving, as he always does, well-known bits of latter-day local history and incident into his pages, often only thinly disguised, he describes the workings of a gang of "firebugs," and later on the trial of a besmirched police Captain. From these scenes he turns to a Patriarch's ball at Delmonico's and shows the world of fashion at its height. The "smart set" flits across the pages. . . . It is a mimic world that these men and women move in, one that in its scenes and primal passions is much like the real world of Gotham.[8]

In 1904, after Fawcett's death, the *Bookman* commented upon his novels with reference to the same standard of photographic Realism. Fawcett's aptitude for detailed reproduction of the actual was the only manifest concern of the evaluation. It was the critic's opinion that "Mr. Fawcett's knowledge of the slums was at best superficial, and when he essayed to write of low life in *The Evil That Men Do,* he failed to impress the modern reader." But, the writer added, *A New York Family* was "one of his best novels" because "he brought in Hoboken and Greenpoint as backgrounds, and his description of the latter remains the very best to be found in fiction. . . . Perhaps none of his books was more entertaining than *Social Silhouettes,* a series of sketches of types, which is well worth re-reading for itself, and which will be found invaluable to any one who wishes to reconstruct a certain period of New York life." The post-mortem estimate concluded with the judgment that Fawcett deserved to be remembered "for his genuine effort to describe life as he saw it and to make use of American material at a time when it was not fashionable to do so."[9]

The Realistic elements in Fawcett's novels elicited favorable comment during his lifetime, too. Some three and one-half months after their initial review of *New York,* the *New York Times* presented another critique of the novel and the novelist. The reflections were more penetrating, but the favorable judgment, other than that it was more forthrightly presented, had not changed— the truth of detail within the novel still commanded respect:

And so few writers are so well equipped as Mr. Fawcett, both by the clearness of his perceptions and by the whole trend of his literary work, to follow M. Zola's perilous example, and to gather the results of his long observation and experience into a novel bearing the title of the great world city of the Western Hemisphere. Yet, as in even M. Zola's case, the title of necessity promises and implies too much. Rome and Lourdes have each its distinctive cachet; but who can compress New York and Paris into the limits of a single novel? New

York is of all faiths—and of none. It is a Northern city, a Western
city, a Southern city, a foreign city. It is a city of the extremes of
selfishness and of philanthropy. . . . There is political New York, in
itself a theme as huge and as repulsive as the monster Frankenstein.
There is educational New York, more and more a gracious and per-
meating force. There is bohemian New York, unique and fascinating,
as Miss Glasgow has dramatically depicted it. There is the greatest
New York of all, the New York of stress and struggle, whose energies
are unceasingly bent upon solving that most elusive of problems, how
to "make both ends meet," and below all, as in every great city, is
the vast, mysterious, awful gulf of utter poverty, of nameless sin, of
crime that knows no law save that of fear. . . .
And how pack all this into one book? Yet Mr. Fawcett has very
nearly done it. The released convict problem, the race problem, the
immigration problem, the problem of the classes and the masses;
international marriage, "the curse of caste," the "vile civic conditions,"
that have made so much of our municipal government a hissing and
a reproach, the iniquity of the cold-blooded self-righteousness that
holds back its skirts from suffering and sin—of all these things and of
many more does Mr. Fawcett write in strong words and wise and
eloquent withal.[10]

III *The Moral Response*

The Realistic novel's adherence to detail and its accurate repre-
sentation of movement were the immediate concern of the individual reviewer; nevertheless, a reviewer's personal taste frequently
influenced his judgment of a work. Evaluation was as much a manifestation of a critic's sensibility as it was a display of his critical
faculty. The Realistic achievement of *New York* impressed the
New York Times critic, but his opinion was equally molded by the
moral tone of the work. He held that, "whether or not 'New York'
becomes a successful book, its readers will find it a true and sug-
gestive one, and the wider that circle of readers the wider will be
an influence that 'makes for righteousness.' " On the other hand,
since the heroine was not a model girl—she was a possible force for
ill—he questioned the propriety of Fawcett's characterization:

The characters are firmly and clearly drawn, though we are con-
strained to protest against the heroine, Doris. Novelists are very
fond of creating such young women, a law unto themselves, a reproach to worldly parents and guardians. Should these writers' own
sisters or daughters walk in the ways of their supposedly perfect

heroines, great would be the consternation, prompt would be the re-
straining edict to hold the young girls back from their adventurous
and dangerous paths. Doris is charming on the printed page but
clothe her in flesh and she would be as "difficult," it is to be hoped
as impossible, as the young Marcella. Such portrayals may make older
readers smile, but to the imitative and willful girls they are distinctly harmful.

Moral considerations also prompted the *New York Times*'s commentary on *A Man's Will*. This time, Fawcett was on the side of
the angels; for the reviewer welcomed the novel as a weapon in the
cause of temperance:

Mr. Fawcett writes this romance with a purpose, just as does Mr.
Besant, and the cause of temperance has found in Mr. Fawcett a
warm advocate. . . . The lesson this story teaches is that a man who
is inclined to drink, to whom the taking of a single drop of alcohol
means inability to stop until he has reached the lowest depth of
human degradation, must never take that first drop. It is then and
only then that the will comes into play. Nothing is more difficult
than to fight this first battle, but fight it a man must. Utter, absolute
abstemiousness is a moral and physical necessity to such, or over-
board go life, health, strength, and position. Mr. Fawcett's romance
is realistic.[11]

The *Nation*'s reviewer of the same novel was able to disengage
his critical intellect from his moral persuasion. His sympathy for
the cause of the novel did not prevent his discerning what he considered to be its lack of artistic merit; he established the separate
drifts at the outset of his review: "Inasmuch as Mr. Fawcett has
lent his brain and pen to the cause of temperance, he is to be ap-
plauded; and inasmuch as he has made a repetitious and dreary
novel, he is to be forgiven. Some day, perhaps, the novel will be
written which shall do for temperance what 'Uncle Tom's Cabin'
did for anti-slavery, what 'Nicholas Nickleby' did for the cause of
kindness. Perhaps, till Fiction has set her mighty engine in motion,
Philanthropy will lack her best ally. All honor to Mr. Fawcett for
the attempt, failure though it is."[12]

Quite often, the result of the disengagement of the moral faculty
from the esthetic consideration took a different turn; frequently,
Fawcett's artistic ability to reflect life favorably impressed the
reviewer, and the theme or subject matter disturbed him. The *New*

EDGAR FAWCETT

York Times reviewer of *A Gentleman of Leisure* remarked with evident approval that "a very fair and somewhat glowing account is given of New-York clubs and balls. Under fictitious names, mostly Dutch in their make-up, many well-known persons, male and female are depicted not untruthfully—Mrs. Spencer Vanderhoff being especially easy to locate." But the *Times* reviewer then questioned the taste of such authentic reproduction, for "in order to heighten the flavor no little injustice is done to persons whose friends cannot fail, if the book comes in their way, to recognize the portraits. Personality of this kind seems hardly worth the candle, in view of the slightness of the work; yet the day is realistic in tendency, and possibly only realism is palatable." [13]

There is no question but that Realistic writings were the vigorous literary expression of the day; but the very Realistic turn of Fawcett's novels proved to be too vivid for the delicate tastes of many reviewers and, ultimately, provoked their condemnation of his fiction. "*Ellen Story* . . . is an ill-painted picture of an ill-chosen theme," railed the reviewer for *Harper's New Monthly Magazine*.[14] "It is difficult to imagine," mourned the *Critic,* "how Edgar Fawcett who put some good work into 'An Ambitious Woman,' could have degenerated so as to write such hopeless stuff as is contained in his latest novel, 'A New York Family.' . . . It is bad enough to have to read the doings of Tammany in the morning papers without taking them up in fiction, too." [15] The *Nation* raised its voice in behalf of taste: "We should feel inclined to call it [*Bressant,* a novel by Julian Hawthorne] the worst novel in our list this week if it were not that we have just been obliged, in the way of duty, to read Mr. Edgar Fawcett's 'Purple and Fine Linen,' which might more justly bear the title of 'Scarlet and Dirty Linen.' " [16]

The review of *Tinkling Cymbals,* in *Lippincott's Monthly Magazine,* warned that "liberal as have been the concessions to modern heroines in the way of enabling them to dismiss pleasing traditions, we must venture to suggest that in the case of Miss Leah Romilly the final limit has been reached." [17] The *Independent* reviewer of *New York* was upset by the novel because the scenes were "too frankly pictured. The depravity of certain quarters of New York, the absolute corruption of the police, the brutality of tenement-house landlords, and a thousand and one phases of squalor, immorality and filth are photographed in minutest detail." [18]

Many reviewers obviously did not share William Dean Howells's conviction that the writer, like the scientist, had to commit himself to the examination of the least significant details. The theoretical preferences of the reviewers are not at issue here, however, nor is their understanding of literary theory a matter of present moment. Their critical comments reveal a groping to apply the tenets of Realistic literary thought to specific works, and the ferment of these expressions is what is of consequence, since it created a charged atmosphere that was conducive to the maturation of a serious literature. In fact, the entire body of Fawcett criticism—whether concerned with the literary structure of his novels, characterization, style, thought, or Realistic expression—manifests a violent intensity that played a vital part in the vivification of American letters.

The critical commentary, by generally dismissing Fawcett from consideration as a major writer, established his position of minor importance on the American literary scene. The fact that most of the commentary was topical, however, and relevant to the literary controversy of the time, suggests that Fawcett's novels were, as has been noted, part of a vigorous literary movement. Just as the reviewers were striving to infuse a new literary theory into their criticism, Fawcett was attempting to translate the same theory into art. The critics found him to be wanting, but the substance of their criticism placed him in the same literary current that contributed so much to the formation of the Realistic novels of such writers as Stephen Crane, Hamlin Garland, Frank Norris, Jack London, and Theodore Dreiser.

CHAPTER 5

The Realistic and Naturalistic Novels and The Matter of Literary Influence

L ITERARY influence is a very subtle happening. Unless there is explicit statement or direct evidence to the effect of its existence, it remains a shadowy and impalpable phenomenon. Yet, what one often intuits or suspects in the way of influencing forces is as significant, if not as substantial, as that which can be proved. Edgar Fawcett's novels, for example, did most vitally influence the works of Hamlin Garland; and this influence is provable.[1] On the other hand, there is no evidence to suggest that Fawcett's novels directly influenced those of Crane, Norris, London, and Dreiser; but they surely helped to shape them and pave the way for them just as certainly as they did Garland's.

The novels of the prominent Realists did not spontaneously erupt upon the literary scene. There was a foreground; and, since Fawcett—the most prolific Realistic writer of his time—was, in essence, the foreground, his pioneering works had to have been instrumental in molding the literary directions of these writers. At the very least, it is apparent that Fawcett's concern with similar settings, incidents, and themes, and his uninterrupted stream of publication, helped to keep a literary movement alive long enough to culminate in the writings of these other men.

By far the most significant number of Fawcett's novels were written and published before those of the major Realistic authors. These men were all contemporaries, however, and it is therefore not strange to find, in looking for specific parallels, that on occasion the major work preceded Fawcett's contribution. Crane's *Maggie*, for example, was popularly published in 1896; and Fawcett's novel, *New York*, did not appear until 1898—but *The Evil That Men Do*, one of Fawcett's earlier tenement novels, appeared in 1889, some seven years before *Maggie*. There are few differences in the two novels, as they share the same artistic purpose and manner. Neither author provides an exit for his characters nor relieves the intensity of his action, and Fawcett brings as much detail to those sections of *The Evil That Men Do* that portray the dispossessed as Crane does to those passages in *Maggie* that reflect the inhabitants of his slum environment. Also, the conditions of life are the same for the characters in both novels—and imbrutement is the common consequence of those conditions.

Environmental forces that shape human destiny and the circumstance of chance that impresses itself upon human movement are the powers to be reckoned with in Fawcett's *Miriam Balestier,* published twelve years before Dreiser's *Carrie,* eight years before Crane's *Maggie,* and three years before Garland's *Main-Travelled Roads*. Forces beyond her control sweep Miriam to her fate with no less sway than they propel Carrie from desire to desire, than they carry Maggie to her inevitable death, than they force Garland's migrant workers from one parcel of land to the next. There is a deterministic universe in all four novels.

Fawcett disparages the values and experiences of the plutocrats in *A Hopeless Case* (1880) with less incision and power than London does in *Martin Eden* (1909), but the views and ends are similar. Correspondences also exist between Fawcett's novels and Frank Norris's. Norris is the greater artist, but Fawcett's indictment of political corruption in *A New York Family* (1891) and the power of wealth in *Tinkling Cymbals* (1884) precedes Norris's condemnation of these same forces in *The Octopus* (1901).

The touchpoints are endless and can be catalogued indefinitely. An analysis of Fawcett's Realistic and Naturalistic novels, however, establishes the relationship in a much more convincing manner, illuminates the substance of Fawcett's novels, and suggests the debt owed to this writer by those who followed him.

I *The Society Novels*

The plot of Fawcett's second published novel,[2] *Purple and Fine Linen* (1873),[3] moves as though it were the archetype of melodramatic manipulation. The beautiful and pure Helen Jeffreys marries the rake, Fuller Dobell, whose heart is in the clutches of the beautiful, but notorious, Edith Everdell. Dobell is wounded in a duel

with the noble friend of the family, Melville Delano, and is brought
to Everdell's house to recuperate. Helen enters the premises disguised as a nurse; her masquerade succeeds, and she proceeds to
expose Everdell's treachery and to win back her husband's love.

Fawcett seldom deviated from a melodramatic plot formula, although in his later novels he overcame the artificiality of contrived
action by subordinating the mechanics of plot to the details of
Realistic description and happening. In *Purple and Fine Linen*,
however, there is little redeeming worth other than in the novel's
diary form, which occasionally reveals Fawcett's intention of chron-
icling external detail and, at the same time, revealing internal motivation. The technique is effective for the first two chapters as a
tantalizing double vision emerges—what Helen reveals in her diary
establishes her movements and her self-image, but the tone of the
entries suggests that Fawcett is mocking the situations that are so
lightly recorded, but so seriously acted by the players. Fawcett does
not sustain this satiric touch, however, and the novel soon degen-
erates into nothing more than a humorless recording of Helen's
involvement in melodramatic situations.

Purple and Fine Linen does not survive its dull and heavy plot;
but, as an early work, one written when Fawcett was twenty-five,
it manifests an interest that was to become the central concern of
Fawcett's later novels—the thematic attack upon the New York
aristocracy of wealth that Fawcett continued in *A Hopeless Case*
(1880),[4] a slender work but exceedingly honest in its plot
development. Never once in the novel does Fawcett force his
heroine, Agnes Wolverton, into an action that is inconsistent with
her character and understanding for the sake of achieving a palatable resolution. In some of his other novels, he compromised the
strength of his theme by forcing his protagonist to embrace the
very values he or she had been warring against throughout the
greater part of the action, but not so with Agnes Wolverton; she
maintains her integrity of purpose to the very end of the novel.

The novel begins as Agnes leaves the Brooklyn home of her aunt
and uncle, the Cliffes, with whom she had been living since the
death of her parents; she goes to Manhattan to stay with her cousins, the Van Corlears, who are most respected members of the
reigning aristocracy. The novel ends as Agnes leaves New York to
rejoin the Cliffes, who have since traveled west. In between these
two movements lies the substance of the novel: Agnes's initiation

into New York society and her subsequent disenchantment. She had anticipated coming into contact with writers, artists, thinkers—the "best people"—but instead she finds that only those of wealth and appropriate lineage are permitted entry into the select circle. She had hoped to find people of honest manner, but instead she learns that the existence of the group is predicated upon the lie that they are innately better than all other people on the face of the earth. Where she had expected a liberality of view, she encountered dogmatism; where she had looked for intellectual stimulation, she discovered superficial badinage only. Achievement, in this milieu, was dependent upon one's dancing ability, one's propensity for the banal, and one's ability to affect an attitude of polite, but bored, nonchalance. The enthusiasm of honest emotion and the desire for cultural enrichment counted for nothing; they were looked upon as evidences of a crude nature and of one not to the manner born.

When Agnes renounces this existence of affectation in order to rejoin the Cliffes, she explains the reasons for her decision to her cousin, Augusta:

I want you to understand just why I am going. It's half because you and those about you belong to another world from mine. Yours is a world that laughs and enjoys itself a great deal, that reads little, thinks little, and is very careless of tomorrow. It is an exceedingly dainty world, with no sympathies for what lies beyond its limits, no interests that do not concern its present amusements. It sets large store by its exclusive selectness; it is elegant, patrician, high bred. I like much of it from an outward point of view, but there is much that from an inward point of view wearies and disheartens me. I want less repression, more genuineness, warmer impulse, wider intellectual reach. I cannot find it here; I can find nothing here that feeds what early education has taught me to believe my better longings.[5]

The meaning of Agnes's speech is lost upon Augusta, precisely because her life has become as self-centered as that of the society that spawned her. She is incapable of understanding any thought that has not been nurtured within the confines of her own effete society:

But that she [Agnes] should calmly renounce its superabundant advantages, after once having experienced them, was beyond conception. To Mrs. Leroy, in that immensity of self-satisfaction with which she had for years surveyed her social surroundings, it seemed that fate had enviably lifted her above a vast aspiring throng. With an absurd miscalculation, she overestimated the number of those who jealously viewed her prosperity. During her girlhood she had been courted; during the brilliant sovereignty of her married days she had constantly known what it was to have her countenance and favor sought with zeal by those who believed it precious. She had always been a great lady in her way, but she made the mistake that, because a few limited hundreds flocked about her with admiring homage, an unseen majority of thousands longed to show her equal allegiance. The multiformity of human ambition was a fact that did not enter her consciousness. She had a pleasant, half-formed conviction that nearly everybody desired a place in her visiting-book.[6]

Agnes Wolverton's move to the West had to be prompted by the same feeling Mark Twain instilled in Huckleberry Finn five years later—she was afraid that cousin Augusta was going to adopt and "sivilize" her, and she couldn't stand it. Agnes, as it turns out, is not the hopeless case of the novel's title; New York society is.

II *The American Dream*

It is but a short stop to move from an indictment of New York society to an attack against the perversion of the American Dream, and the connection between the two was apparent to Fawcett. The spirit of the American Dream promised an end to the caste system, a leveling of society to the point of equal treatment for all, and the establishment of an environment that would be conducive to the development of an unconstrained psychological and economic freedom for the individual. The values of New York society ran counter to this spirit. In an otherwise undistinguished novel, *The Adventures of a Widow* (1884),[7] Fawcett had his protagonist, Pauline Van Corlear, make the connection: " 'Do you know what New York means? It means what America means—or what America *ought* to mean, from Canada to the Gulf! And that is—exemption from the hateful bonds of self-glorifying snobbery which have disgraced Europe for centuries! You call yourself an aristocrat. How dare you do so? You dwell in a land which was washed with the blood, less than a century ago, of men who died to kill just what you boast of and exalt!' "[8]

The Adventures of a Widow merely touches the problem of wealth and democracy, of aristocracy and the Dream. It briefly calls attention to its existence, and then it fades into the nether world of romance. *Tinkling Cymbals*,[9] published in the same year, however, contains Fawcett's strongest condemnation of the American plutocrats and his sharpest criticism of those who perverted the spirit and substance of the Dream. Fawcett began other novels with the same apparent resolve to castigate the manners and values of the American ruling class, but the glitter of their wealth seemed to dazzle him, and his attack faded into apology long before the novel's end.

Tinkling Cymbals is not one of these novels; like *A Hopeless Case*, it makes no brief with the spirit of compromise, and its strength resides in its unswerving purpose. Lawrence Rainsford, the political theoretician of the novel, voices the theme of the work and, by extension, the social consciousness of America. His remarks are stirring and militant; they sound the warning of the nation's conscience:

These exclusionists, who base their assumptions of superiority on the shadow they call birth or the substance they call wealth, deserve an unqualified censure. They are the curse of our republic; in a manner they threaten its advancement and its prosperity. They are a taint in its rich young blood, and they mean a chronic malady whose development must work incalculable harm. . . . Aristocracy has no right of existence within this land. The frauds and corruptions in our politics are not one-half so perilous as this other rapidly-increasing ill. Our dishonest state-craft has sprung, after all, from democracy itself; democracy, who is responsible for it, may one day cure it with her own medicines. But this aping of what had its rise long ago in the dark feudal ages of Europe—tis subservience to a vicious and degrading vanity—this open and cruel sneer at the very laws by which our country must either shape her destiny or perish—ah! that is quite another matter! The great social inequalities of our uncompleted civilization are lamentable enough; but education is always waging her war against these, and it is not a millennial dream to trust that she may one day vastly modify if she does not wholly annul them. But when pretentious braggarts have succeeded in making new social inequalities, feeding the bigotry which applauds them upon their own hoarded capital, what shall prevent the national spirit itself from sinking to a level with this disastrous change? Our government will lapse into monarchism—that poisonous nourishment on which the patrician idea has in all times most malignantly thriven. There is not a very wide step between the monopolist of millions who drives a pompous drag up Fifth Avenue and the miscalled "nobleman" who has received from his king the preposterous hereditary right of making a country's laws. To my own ears there is an ominous mutter of revolutionary bloodshed at this very hour in our land. I sometimes almost wish that such calamity might fall upon us quickly, if any vital good were to follow. Yet revolutions too often accomplish nothing save ruin. Meanwhile the luxuriously selfish class yearly grows larger. American society, as it is called, is no longer provincial; the day for declaring it so is past. People come to us from European courts and marvel at the scale of splendor on which our revelries are conducted. We are foreign and imitative only in our snobbery—and perhaps, I might add, our immorality.[10]

Leah Romilly, the protagonist of *Tinkling Cymbals*, is the daughter of Elizabeth Cleeve Romilly, a woman who had platformed vigorously in her youth on questions of public reformation. Leah, in rebellion against her mother's values, marries Tracy Tremaine, the wealthy scion of an aristocratic family. She soon becomes disenchanted with her new life, in which "the people think and talk such trivialities"; and she likens this shimmering world to "the palace of the Sleeping Beauty, with the inmates wakened after a hundred years of slumber. The world has gone rolling on, and they have known nothing about it."[11] Leah finally leaves her husband; and, under the tutelage of Lawrence Rainsford, she finds freedom, meaning, and a new love.

Leah's Sleeping Beauty analogy stirs up the excitement of the novel, for what makes the excesses of the privileged class so horrendous is that they are committed at a time when there is a feel of great social change in the air. Fawcett establishes the progressive climate of the era early in the novel when he says of Mrs. Romilly: "Ridicule, disrespect, calumny, no longer shot at her a single shaft. She had outlived all that; a new generation was supplanting the old; tolerance and liberality had begun to set her deeds in their proper light before men. Massive prejudice still existed; she saw it in its full, burly bulk, and deplored it with a gentle, dignified sorrow. At the same time she felt that the air of the age had cleared wonderfully, so to speak; in religion, in morality, in charitable administration, there seemed to her a precious and thrifty enlightenment. Her imperishable optimism rejoiced and exulted."[12]

The existence of a plutocracy within a current of democratic social change is anachronistic. That is the point of Rainsford's speech, and the novel dramatically reveals the resultant tension as it constantly forces the two worlds into violent collision. When Tremaine shows Leah the sights of Newport, she responds to the beauty of the natural surroundings by calling to mind a less pleasant sight: "There is a cruelty of luxury about these cliffs, as you call them. They are *too* lovely. I mean that while so many people are shut in hot garrets, not knowing where they shall get their next crust, all this pomp and comfort seems like an injustice,— an outrage!"[13]

In its way, *Tinkling Cymbals* offers as sharp a critique of the failure of the American Dream as Walt Whitman's *Democratic Vistas;* indeed, the thought of the two works is markedly similar. In *Vistas,* Whitman wrote that "The United States are destined either to surmount the gorgeous history of feudalism, or else prove the most tremendous failure of time"; and in *Tinkling Cymbals,* Rainsford rails against "this aping of what had its rise long ago in the dark feudal ages of Europe . . . this open and cruel sneer at the very laws by which our country must either shape her destiny or perish." The note of present pessimism and future optimism also finds expression in the two works. Whitman looked his time "searchingly in the face" and was sickened to death by the corruption, hypocrisy, and shallowness he viewed in American life. He lamented the failures of the present, but he managed to project hope for a time when "first-class poets, philosophs, and authors" would mold the creative character of the nation.

At the conclusion of *Tinkling Cymbals,* Rainsford also takes a dim view of the present, but he cautions Leah not to be too impatient with the nation's lack of cultural progress and with its dearth of outstanding poets. Such development, he maintains, "are not possible in this new land of ours," and then, echoing Whitman, he prophesies that "we need at least a century to make them so—if we live a century longer as the republic we have aimed to be. Brilliant men and women will meanwhile rise among us; not a few such as have already risen. But a wide diffusion of just that special humanity to which you refer is yet a future gain."[14]

III *Experimentation in Style*

Purple and Fine Linen marked the beginning of Fawcett's thematic attack upon the abuses of New York society and the extension of that concern to his interest in the Dream of American democracy; it also signaled his early interest in the intricacies of literary point of view and his penchant for experimentation with the novel form, a tendency very much in keeping with the nature of the Realistic literary movement and very much in evidence in another of his early novels, *Ellen Story* (1876),[15] the structure of which is shockingly modern.

In *Ellen Story,* Fawcett sets his characters through their rather conventional paces; but he moves them in double time, and, thus, the vision one has of them is never static, but a fluid composite of a number of active images. It is no great matter in the novel that Archibald Howard falls in love with Ellen Story and she with him, that they suffer through the traditional lovers' misunderstandings, and that they overcome all difficulties by story's end. What these characters do is of relatively little importance; the significance of action is to be found in *why* they do and in the startling presentation of the doing itself.

Fawcett presents the story from three different points of view, and the chapters are appropriately headed, "He Narrates," "She Narrates," and "The Author Narrates." Thus in the first chapter, "He Narrates," Howard writes a letter to a friend explaining how he came to meet Ellen. He had grown weary of the constant round of tedious society affairs; and, to amuse himself and to stimulate some interest in his life, he had wagered with a few friends that he could gain the approval of his peers for a girl who held neither wealth nor position simply by escorting her to a number of fashionable affairs.

In Chapter 2, "She Narrates," Ellen relates the circumstances of her life prior to meeting Howard; and in Chapter 3, "The Author Narrates," Fawcett details the first meeting of the two and offers a second insight into motivation. It seems that Archibald had not made the wager with his friends out of boredom with life, but out of curiosity with self: "No; the only thing that has ever induced him to notice Jack Vandervoort's and Robbie Roscoe's absurd bet has been curiosity. This alone. He wants to find out whether or no it be in his power to do this thing. It is very much like not feeling just sure whether one can leap a certain ditch of a certain width without one's trousers coming to miry grief. Does a fellow think anything more of such a question after he has settled it? Surely not; but *until* settled it bothers him a trifle."[16]

By superimposing his omniscient awareness upon a character's limited knowledge of self, Fawcett strips his character bare and exposes the self-deception of human rationalizations. He constantly provides a double vision of thought and action, and he places moral judgment of character in the complex world of ambiguity. After Ellen resolves to remain indifferent to the attractions of social fortune, the author narrates:

> We know this girl's philosophy. . . . Or rather we know how she had philosophized regarding certain special events—how she had told herself that if Archie Howard's whim should change in a week or in three days, she would snap her fingers in fortune's face and go back resignedly to her rocks, her poetry and her solitude.
>
> Well whether she would have done this or not (and you will very much doubt whether she would . . .), Elly had nevertheless firmly convinced herself that she only found in her good fortune a huge amusement; and therefore a belief in her own utter indifference as to her own social future may have given her manner a careless little touch that just rightly blended with its other features.[17]

Fawcett's presentation of events penetrates different levels of consciousness and illuminates the wide gap that exists between what seems and what is. He adds to this probing of human action a disintegration of time, which can best be understood in terms of modern literary efforts to collapse the past and the future, memory and desire, into the present moment and thereby suggest the simultaneity of all happening, the universality of all experience.[18] The "He Narrates" chapters are written in the past tense. They are somewhat reflective; and, since they are written at a time when the action has already concluded (a future time from the perspective of the action itself), they implicitly assure some sort of satisfactory resolution to the dilemmas of the plot. On the other hand, the "She Narrates" chapters are written in the present tense (which is time past from Howard's perspective); and they therefore offer a sense of immediacy, excitement, suspense, and heightened involvement. The reader is moved backward and forward, into and out of the action, until the dilations settle into the present time of the author, who narrates with an omniscience that transcends time.

There is a cyclical pattern to *Ellen Story*, for Fawcett's manipulation of time brings the reader back full circle to the internal probing of human action—to the concern for psychological understanding of behavior. Ellen's sections, because they occur in the immediacy of the present, quite often assume the form of interior monologue, and, thus, a triple vision results, the substance of which is shaped by what Ellen says aloud to other characters, by the presentation of her socially inhibited thoughts—what she truly thinks—and by what Fawcett, the author-narrator, knows to be true about her.

IV Realism à la the Scientist and the Toad

Fawcett's experimentation with the novel form was in keeping with the spirit of William Dean Howells's Realistic credo. No set of events, Howells insisted, was too insignificant to be accorded literary attention; and it followed that no stylistic technique was too radical to be discouraged in the pursuit of human truth. Fawcett's novels, however, contributed to the Realistic movement in matters of substance as well as of style; they were steeped in descriptive detail; they probed social problems; they frequently examined lower-class manners; and they dissected man's existence with the clinical detachment of a scientist.

A Man's Will (1888)[19] is of slight literary merit, but it is in keeping with the spirit of Realism. Fawcett took himself too seriously in this novel with a purpose, and the result is a novel without humor —a tract—warning against the evils of alcohol. Johnston Saltonstall, a loving husband, devoted father, respected financier, and irredeemable alcoholic is killed one night in a tawdry barroom brawl while in a drunken stupor. The novel follows the life of his son, Edmund, and chronicles his attempts to overcome his strong desire for drink. Edmund's life follows the pattern of his father's, but the son ultimately wins his struggle as he comes under the care of Dr. Alsop, who treats his affliction as a disease and thereby convinces him that his problem is not hereditary. Dr. Alsop makes Edmund understand that alcoholism is caused by physiological as well as psychological imbalances; and he cautions him to refrain from all drink, for, as with all addicts, the cure rests with the strength of the patient's will and his ability to frustrate completely the demands of his habit.

There are descriptive passages of sheer fantasy in the novel; but, interestingly enough, Fawcett employed them with Realistic intent.

Edmund's sleepless nights occasion this Realism of the imagination and so, too, do his seizures of delirium tremens:

> By this time he had reached the farther end of the room, and with his form close-pressed against the wall he stared at the table. What dark shape was that gliding toward him? It was the same creature that he had seen ambushed between the bottle and the glasses. But it was far longer than it had seemed there. Its flat head was lifted as it advanced; its eyes burned like two small, lurid coals; its forked tongue began to flicker. Then, with a motion that was instantaneous, it drew itself up into a tremulous ring, having part of its body curved above like the neck of a black swan. Seeing that it was about to strike, Edmund sprang sideways. But he could not elude it; a second later he felt its fangs in his flesh and its length of clammy shape twisted pell-mell all over his hands and arms. But even then, just as he was about to utter a mad cry of anguish the phantom faded, and he knew that it had been a phantom only.[20]

The story is little more than campaign literature, but, in keeping with the Realistic current in Fawcett's fiction, the novel, unlike Walt Whitman's *Franklin Evans* and the hundreds of other romantic temperance novels, approaches the problem of alcoholism with clinical detachment. In what he deemed to be the spirit of scientific investigation, Fawcett examined the physiological, psychological, and hereditary impulses that medical opinion had pronounced to be the causal factors of the disease. Though Fawcett strayed often in the novel and indulged in the bathos of melodrama, he never departed significantly from the Realistic intent of the work. He established the spirit of his intent in the dedication, and the spirit permeated the entire Saltonstall affair: "To my friend Dr. William A. Hammond, whose high intellectual gifts almost tempt me to forget them while I recall his generous and humane heart, I dedicate, in sincere loyalty, this faulty and unequal story, yet one for which his great medical and scientific experience may perhaps find some justifying parallel."

A New York Family (1891)[21] is another Realistic novel, although a curious one. It purports to be many things but ultimately resolves itself into little more than a maudlin, melodramatic appeal to sentimental taste. The novel deals with the fortunes and heartbreaks of the Everard family, and it comes complete with an Horatio Alger protagonist; a faithful, understanding, and enduring wife; a near "fallen woman"; an alcoholic son in the clutches of a woman of the world; a daughter who scorns the simple but honest manner of her parents and is seduced by the glitter of wealth; another son whose values are tainted by the lure of easy money; and, finally, a happy ending, in which the Everard family members recount their misfortunes but count their blessings and rejoice in their love for one another.

For all its melodramatic horrors, A New York Family is a curious piece inasmuch as Fawcett attempted two things of serious design in the novel. He tried—and failed—to invest the work with Naturalistic undertones, and he attempted—and succeeded—to blend his fictional story with the historical pattern of contemporary happenings. The Naturalistic suggestion makes its appearance early in the novel. Three deaths occur within the first two chapters: Everard's father dies first, followed by his wife's father, and then by their infant son. In a short paragraph, Everard questions the order of things in the universe, the unimportance of man, the impermanence of life, and the beneficence of nature. The tone of the paragraph is similar to the note struck by Henry Adams when he speculated upon the meaning of life after the sudden death of his sister; and it has much in common both with the musings of the correspondent in Crane's "The Open Boat" and with Presley's reaction to the senseless killing of his friends in Norris's The Octopus. But Fawcett merely introduces the speculation and then deserts it; the philosophical questioning never becomes an integral part of the work. It does reappear from time to time; but, since its appearance is sporadic and not of a piece with the novel's purpose, its presence is incongruous, and it does nothing to redeem for the novel its sense of high intention.

The Naturalistic elements thus fail to satisfy, but the Realistic segments of the novel emerge in an interesting manner and are brilliantly fashioned. Midway through the story, Everard's oldest son, Frederick, engages in a scheme to blackmail Boss Tweed, the political czar of New York. At this point, the threads of the melodramatic story line are dropped; and, in what appears to be a strange development, the world of fiction moves into the world of fact. Fawcett had prepared for this new movement somewhat earlier in the novel when he had Bertha, Frederick's sister, catch a glimpse of Jim Fisk, the Gilded Age's dashing robber baron, while vacationing at Saratoga.

Fisk appeared only for a moment, but in the chapters concerned with Frederick's corruption, some five in all, Fawcett introduces an entire gallery of historical figures. He exposes the Tammany affairs of Boss Tweed and his henchman, Peter Sweeny. He blends into the scene such corrupt officials as Connolly, Woodward, Watson, O'Brien, Morrissey, and Judge Barnard—all members of Tweed's ring. In broad strokes, he sets forth the rascality of the Crédit Mobilier affair; the duplicity of elected officials; the apathy of the public; the muckraking opposition of the *New York Times;* the telling effect of Thomas Nast's political cartoons (in fact, these chapters are liberally illustrated with many of Nast's drawings); the overthrow of the Tweed rule; and the escape, extradition, and death of Tweed in the Ludlow Street Jail. The Gilded Age, in all of its acquisitiveness, emerges in these chapters.

Fawcett makes use of this Realistic scene to reinforce the thematic substance of the novel. Frederick's involvement with the Tweed ring adds a touch of historical authenticity to his portrait and actions, and his presence in the midst of members of this group endows the historical personages with a vibrant dramatic reality. His fall is made all the more convincing and understandable when viewed in the context of the political, economic, and moral corruption of the Gilded Age. With the corrupting influences in the world of the novel heightened by those in the world without the novel, the inevitability of Frederick's descent is an unalterable dictate; and the weaving together of the two worlds is of significance in the development of Realistic fiction.

Fawcett returned to the New York scene again in *New York* (1898),[22] a Realistic novel that is monumental in scope and ambitious in undertaking. He attempted to telescope the life-and-death movements of the entire city into the pages of this one novel, and the *New York Times* reviews attested to his partial success.[23] As usual with Fawcett's novels, however, the plot of *New York* is weak and the situation contrived.. George Oliver is released from jail as the story opens, and the reader follows him in his tortured attempts to convince society that, despite the error of his immature years, he is an upright, honest young man. He asks only to be judged for what he is, not for what he was. After many trials, he wins his case and proves to those with whom he has come in contact that they have judged him unfairly. At the novel's close, he looks forward to his marriage with Doris Josseleyn, who offers him love and the chance for respectability.

The plot moves in this rather pedestrian fashion, but the strength of the novel lies elsewhere—in its detailed descriptions of the more sordid New York scenes and in its uncompromising penetration of the city's prosperous facade, which reveals the underlying truth of the poverty and the horror that accompany progress. The dedication to Henry James establishes, once again, the serious intent of the work: "With the touch of a Velasquez you have painted many portraits. No living Briton or American ranks above you in your art. And so with reverence for the depth and reach of it, I venture to make you my modest offering, as one to whom your gifts have been for years a delight, and by whom your fame, now strengthening with time, was long ago foretold."

Fawcett covers his canvas of New York in rapid, uneven strokes. He fashions images of Wall Street and of men like Mr. Blashfield, whose stock manipulations affect the destiny of nations; he exposes police corruption from the person of Garrety, the cop on the beat who takes bribes from whiskey sellers and harlots, to Captain Cummisky, whose transgressions involve Tammany politics, reform movements, and elected city officials. With a change of color, a shift of scene, Fawcett varies the pattern of his canvas as he moves the novel from the upper side of the city's movements to the dark underside of its life. He sketches in a trip to a New York prison and, with compassion, sets forth the depraved nature of the inmates; he portrays the bitterness of life for the Negro in an enlightened city; and he unveils the aimless, primitive existence of those who live without hope in the city's lowest depths. Whenever his picture threatens to become too dark, Fawcett extricates it from its murky setting long enough to describe the fresh and natural beauty of New York's Central Park; to comment, in a light vein, upon the timidity of New York theatrical producers; and to satirize the ostentatious manner, the gaudy dress, and the mindless activity of New York's elite.

Fawcett did not allow the novel to remain too long in the upper air, however. *New York* is basically a dark novel, written in keeping with Howells's dictum to the novelist to expose the mean and the commonplace in life. The best moments of the novel do just that, and such scenes as the following compare favorably with similar ones in Crane's *Maggie*:

May had arrived hot and humid, as it so often does in New York. In the east side street life expanded, amplified, deserting its narrow indoor haunts. The sidewalks were populous with ragged children. Innumerable babies were carried here and there in the frail arms of their little sisters. Tiny two-year old shapes tottered about in constant peril of overthrow. The doors of vile taverns were opened, and inside you could catch glimpses of piled barrels and cobwebbed ceilings and grimy floors. Often, too, in the dusk beyond their thresholds you could see the inalienable patron of the "dead house," an old woman, it might be, with snowy hair straggling down over a bloated face, or a man so thin that his filthy garb hung loose round every shrunken limb, either of them lifting to avid lips the five-cent glass of liquor which had death in it, yet a kind of death that for some mocking reason killed slowly. Girls and boys, carrying cans of beer, mounted the stairs of tenements and entered rooms where fettered beds, crawling with vermin, were surmounted by flaring prints of Christ and the Holy Virgin. Brawny men, out of work, would loll at the narrow windows, their hairy breasts half exposed by the sagging undershirt which alone clad their torsos. Pinched, cadaverous women, with sick infants in their arms, would sit on the stoops and shriek stacatto reprimands to others of their offspring whom the slimy gutters too forcibly lured. Along Hester Street, and in parts of Baxter and Bayard Streets, the odors grew sickening as the sudden heat persevered. . . . The first raw discords of the elevated as its trains began to rush past his windows, would wake him. . . . Drunkards, men and women, would totter past him on their homeward routes.[24]

The dismal tableau of *New York* is almost a replica of one Fawcett had created in an earlier tenement novel, *The Evil That Men Do* (1889),[25] a study of poverty, disease, and death. The life of Cora Strang is set forth from her early years as a seamstress to her untimely end—still a young woman—as a derelict on the Bowery. Her meaningless pilgrimage moves upward first, from working girl's home, to maidservant, to counter girl, to mistress, and thence downward through the trials of pregnancy, desertion, abortion, prostitution, and alcoholism to death. There is a realistically detailed background to Cora's movements, replete with scenes of starving families, exploited factory workers, brutal men, harsh landladies, drunken brawls, and consumptive children. The scope of *The Evil That Men Do* is not nearly so broad as in *New York*, but the novel magnifies the seamier side of city life to a degree of intensity that culminates in a moment of terror and in a feeling of revulsion for the depravities of industrial progress.

V *From Realism to Naturalism*

A late nineteenth-century Realistic writer, whose novels were imbedded in the thought and life of his time, could hardly help but emerge as a Naturalistic writer also. It is as Isabel Coggeshal remarks to her novelist father in Fawcett's *The House at High Bridge*: "Oh, papa, you're sometimes a naturalist, too! I read in some magazine, the other day, that realism imbued the very air of this age and that none of our best novelists could help breathing it in."[26] Or, stated another way, writers became Naturalists because Realism was there. Henry Steele Commager, writing of American authors at the turn of the century, observed that "They shamelessly mixed Darwinian biology with Freudian psychology, and blended in contributions from Spencer, Haeckel, Loeb, Nietzsche, Einstein, Pavlov, and Jung to make what passed for a naturalistic brew. They were naturalists, they were determinists, they were behaviorists."[27] Though his particular mixture was not always integrated into the action of his story, Fawcett, whose novels preceded those of the outstanding Naturalistic writers, had concocted his own Naturalistic brew out of the thoughts of these nineteenth-century economists, scientists, philosophers, and psychologists.

VI *The Philosophical Potpourri*

The plot of *A Demoralizing Marriage* (1889)[28] moves mechanically along the route of the already established Fawcett formula. The events of the novel unfold with an ease of familiarity—with a sense of having been there before. There are glimpses of fashionable life, references to the pathos of impoverished existence, discussions of cultural import, dilemmas of choice, and resolutions of integrity. Rosalind Maturin, who, along with her sister, has inherited six million dollars from her father's estate, is interested in the new ideas of the day—agnosticism, skepticism, and evolution. She falls in love with Carroll Remington, however, and marries this attractive but intellectually shallow darling of the social set. Within two years of the marriage, she becomes disenchanted with the frothy world of vacuity; and she sues Carroll for divorce after she finds out that he has been unfaithful to her. Fortunately, for all concerned, Carroll dies; and Rosalind is free to marry Cyril Trelawney in time to aid him in the writing of his book, A *Universal History of Skepticism.*

Fawcett has again created a most uninspiring sequence of events, but he has once more managed to infuse the action with the serious thought of his day. Rosalind's Uncle Seth, for example, is a man of simple taste who reacts to nature as an Emersonian Transcendentalist, but who learns from it with the humility characteristic of Thoreau. He receives all of his ideas, he says, "from watching the sun and the clouds and the stars and the trees and the crops and the grass . . . from hearing the brooks flow and the birds chirp and the winds sing."[29] Then there is Cyril Trelawney's first wife, Naomi, who looks upon nature as "an immense creator and immense destroyer. She brings us forth and she receives us back again into her bosom. There is nothing but Nature," she insists, "producing and then annihilating, throughout all the big cycles of the centuries."[30]

Uncle Seth develops his insights into human behavior by attuning his soul to the beauties and wonders of natural existence. The pulsations of nature become his model for existence, and he intuitively patterns his life upon her workings. Naomi, on the other hand, elevates nature to godhood and then views her inhuman, indifferent god with scientific detachment. It is Cyril Trelawney's function in the novel to combine the two views and to express Fawcett's own thoughts. Trelawney weds his wife's Scientific Pantheism—there is no other name for it—to Uncle Seth's intuitive apprehensions of nature and arrives at a belief in a personal immortality based upon a Scientific Transcendental understanding of nature. He explains his insights to Rosalind:

Evolution tells me that behind its vast changes, from the simple to the complex and from the homogeneous to the heterogeneous, lurks at least a symbolic conception of some supreme consciousness. These rhythmic waves of development are too mighty not to have emanated from some mightier Sea. In other words, I find God behind nature. Those last are not scientific words,—not the words of an exact thinker, I admit,—and it is a fixed tenet of mine that in exact thought lies the hope of society. Nevertheless, just here I make this concession, as one

might say, to pure sentiment alone. Now, if that Divinity be *beyond*
all the natural manifestations that we witness, I see no reason to imagine that He would have made our intelligences merely mortal. I think
it is almost logical to feel half certain that, as our senses both reveal
to us and conceal from us our material surroundings, in like manner
they both suggest and hide our spiritual ones.[31]

Despite such passages of philosophical speculation, *A Demoralizing Marriage* does not hold together as a Naturalistic novel. The
musings upon nature, death, immortality, and fate are only occasional; they are sounded here and there throughout the novel, but
their import is never fully woven into the action or the theme of
the novel. That is, characters put forth learned theories of man's
controlled destiny, but their own lives move freely without the restrictions of deterministic compulsion. The novel is of interest, however, for it is an early expression—although peripheral and slight—
of Naturalistic considerations in the genre.

In *Outrageous Fortune,* published five years later, in 1894,[32]
Fawcett resumed the same philosophical considerations he had injected into *A Demoralizing Marriage.* The publisher's blurb, ap-
pended to the novel, emphasizes the currency of such matters in
fiction. "There are some fine descriptive passages in the latest work
of Edgar Fawcett," it reads, "much admirable dialogue, sparkling
with wit and humor, and a dash, here and there, of the piquant
materialistic speculation which appears to be so popular nowa-
days."

The publisher's remarks to the contrary, *Outrageous Fortune* succeeds where *A Demoralizing Marriage* had failed, in that Fawcett
does not sprinkle his dashes of thought here and there; instead,
he integrates the Naturalistic contemplations of the characters into
the plot and theme of his story. Basil Moncrieffe, the protagonist
of the novel, views himself as a martyr of destiny, moved in life by
external forces that do not allow him the freedom to assert a willful
choice. Encouraged by his friend, Whitewright, Moncrieffe sets up
his medical practice in Riverview, New York, a small suburban
community of wealth; there he soon realizes that his actions are
determined by his desire to achieve success and recognition and
by his instinctive rather than rational responses to situations. He
falls in love with Eloise Thirlwall, but chance occurrences prevent
him from proposing marriage to her; other chance occurrences

thrust him into the company of the wealthy young socialite, Elma Blagdon; and, in a bewildering moment of confusion, swept by the dictates of circumstance and passion, he agrees to marry her. The marriage is unsuccessful, but there is no way out for Moncrieffe until chance, once more, interferes and changes his destiny. Elma dies, and Moncrieffe, for the first time in his life, experiences a sense of freedom. He quickly marries Eloise before the forces of fate can regroup and shape his life anew.

There are three deaths in the novel—Whitewright's, Elma's, and Mrs. Thirlwall's—and three distinct philosophical attitudes toward death—Whitewright's scientific pessimism, Mrs. Thirlwall's agnosticism, and Eloise's Transcendental apprehension of God and goodness in death. Although Eloise's is the final, affirmative view of the novel, Whitewright's philosophy dominates at the outset. There is no respite in the early pages from his theme of man's individual unimportance, his view that man is no larger than he might look from the top of the highest mountain, from which height, if man could be seen at all, a Newton would not be distinguishable from an idiot. Even at the moment of his death, Whitewright's thought remains unchanged: "How commonplace it seems to die, when one thinks of the billions and billions that have set this fashion for us from remotest centuries down to the present minute."[33]

Whitewright has nothing to affirm in life or in death, but his view of man and his own security in resignation transform Mrs. Thirlwall from an unquestioning theist into a rather reluctant, but rational, agnostic, who finds meaning in questioning. After her confrontations with Whitewright, Mrs. Thirlwall confesses:

Oh yes; I believe now that knowledge is everything. Once I did not. The struggle was terrible with me. I suppose mine is what they call the religious temperament. Faith had meant so much to me. . . . The surrender of a palpable, tangible Revelation cost me a fearful ordeal. Mere reason seemed so cold and aidless after that loving divinity, that providential succour, in which I had trusted implicitly for years! . . . Is it not Huxley who says that the slaying of a beautiful hypothesis by an ugly fact is one of the great tragedies of science? My awakening into rationalism partook of just that tragic element.[34]

Eloise, who remains unmoved by rationalism and unseduced by the romantic forlornness of Whitewright, offers the novel's third philosophical point of view. Her God is hope, her faith is in the divinity of her soul, and her comfort is found in identification with nature. Speaking of Whitewright, she observes that: " 'Both of us have apparently found peace, but in ways that are widely different. He has found it . . . in a conviction of his own complete individual unimportance. *I* have found it in feeling myself doomed to annihilation among the very best of company. Magnus Whitewright spoke truly when he said to me that there is nothing actually less marvelous in the lungs of a gnat than in the brain of a Shakespeare. So, I feel, there is nothing more or less natural in my own bodily decadence than in the wilting of a rose, the plashing of a sea-wave, the fading of a sunset.' " [35]

Basil Moncrieffe does not share in any of these metaphysical speculations; he stands apart and contemplates all with Tennysonian detachment, "holding no creed, yet contemplating all." But, perhaps, this assessment is an oversimplification, for he does have a belief to offer the novel, although not one pertinent to man's spiritual destiny. Moncrieffe is a pessimistic determinist; the notion of free will is absurd to him; in its place, he postulates the force of an evil destiny that subverts man's desires, controls his actions, and charts his unhappy fate. Whitewright, though he asserts the same controlled destiny for man, frequently argues this belief with Moncrieffe; for he cannot accept his friend's dimly pessimistic view of existence. Whitewright maintains that destiny does not tell for evil only but also for good. He agrees with Moncrieffe that the controls of destiny are not in the hands of man; but he insists that the results of fate are accidental and haphazard, not planned, and he argues in substance, in words that are perhaps best expressed in Thomas Hardy's poem, "Hap": "These purblind Doomsters had as readily strown/ Blisses about my pilgrimage as pain."

Just as Eloise's view of man's spiritual immortality triumphs in the novel's metaphysical debate, so, too, does her thesis of positive determinism become dominant in the argument over man's mortal destiny. She counters Moncrieffe's pessimism and Whitewright's ambivalence with a belief that all actions and events ultimately lead to an absolute good. When Moncrieffe's fortune changes, he comes to understand that destiny is for good as well as evil; but he also tends to believe now that all moves toward the good, since, as Eloise insists, all things emanate from the goodness of God. At the end of the story, Moncrieffe is still a determinist; but, in Fawcett's ambiguous Naturalistic brew, he is a positive, or Spencerian, or Transcendental determinist.

VII *Determinism*

Fawcett's scientific and philosophical potpourri is but a peripheral manifestation of the Naturalistic novel. The core of Naturalism is to be found not in tangential and abstract discussions of current thought, but in the philosophy of scientific determinism which is woven into the fictional theme and which establishes the governance of character by economic, environmental, psychological, and hereditary forces. Thus Realism is an esthetic doctrine that concerns itself with attributes of style and subject matter. Metaphysical speculation in the novel is a natural consequence of Realism; and Naturalism, nineteenth-century variety, is the infusion of a thesis—a deterministic thesis—into the Realistic work. The passage, for example, describing the inhabitants of the lower depths in *New York*, is Realistic, but it assumes a Naturalistic attitude when Fawcett contributes his deterministic comment to the effect that these people could not be other than what they were: "The bitter despotisms of birth and environment had allowed them no choice. Their evil had been a necessitous heritage; it would have seemed incredible if they had trodden straight paths when every baleful force of circumstance had dragged them into the zigzags of crooked ones."[36]

This Naturalistic suggestion in *New York* is interesting, but it is not, as it is in *An Ambitious Woman* (1884),[37] a vital concern of the novel. In its broad plot movements, *An Ambitious Woman* closely parallels the action of many of Fawcett's society novels. Claire Twining's father dies; and, when her mother refuses to spend the family's meager savings for a proper burial, Claire, in angry rebellion, leaves her Greenpoint home to seek her fortune in Manhattan. She steadily rises to social prominence as she is taken in by the wealthy Bergemann family; meets people of refinement; marries Harbert Hollister, a Wall Street financier; and eventually becomes the most enchanting society figure in New York life.

Claire's reversal takes place at the height of this success when her husband loses his money, and all that she had labored so long and so hard to cultivate—her position in society—threatens to fade into nothingness. Claire's fall is a fortunate one, however, in the

sense that F. Scott Fitzgerald had in mind when he later propounded that his people of the 1920's lost everything they had in
the boom period. When Claire is stripped of wealth, position, and
self-respect, she comes to understand the destructive nature of her
misdirected ambition and sets about to reclaim her life by seeking
more meaningful values by which to live. Claire's fall is, therefore,
the prelude to her rise; in this respect, Fawcett's *An Ambitious
Woman* anticipates William Dean Howells's *The Rise of Silas Lapham,* published one year later, in which Lapham's purification and
moral elevation coincide with the loss of his wealth.

An Ambitious Woman is ostensibly another Fawcett tale of the
quest for moral values set within the sparkle and glitter of a moneyed
society, but Fawcett had far greater purpose than this for his novel.
The vitality of the work does not exist in Claire's search for meaning
or in its castigation of manners and wealth; it pulsates in its Naturalistic charting of the forces that sweep Claire to her determined
end. The propulsions of environment, heredity, and instinct combine to form the powerful current of the novel; they invest the work
with significance and literary excellence far beyond the claim of its
societal theme.

As nature comes alive in Thomas Hardy's Naturalistic novels to
shape the destiny of his characters, so the environment of Claire
Twining's early surroundings imparts its character to her being. An
excellent and detailed description of Greenpoint in Brooklyn occu-
pies the first three pages of the novel, and its function is less to
present a Realistic setting for action than to suggest the influence
of environment upon character. It is evident that the dull, oppres-
sive nature of her surroundings affects Claire. One either succumbs
to this environment or escapes from it, but one never merely ac-
cepts it. The pervading force of the atmosphere is apparent in the
brief description of the Twinings's second year in Greenpoint:

And so the weeks went by. The bitterness of their second winter in
Greenpoint had now yielded to the mildness of a second spring. But
the vernal change brought no cheer to Claire. In the little yellowish-
drab wooden house where they dwelt, with lumber-yards and sloop-
wharves blocking all view of the river, with stupid, haggling neigh-
bors on either side of them, with ugliness and stagnation and poverty
at arm's reach, was a girl so weighed upon and crushed by the stern
arbitraments of want, that she often felt herself as much a captive as

if she could not have moved a limb without hearing the clank of a chain.[38]

The environment incites in Claire a desire to escape its dehumanizing claim upon human life. Thus, its influence is negative only; it remains for the accident of her birth, the claim of heredity, to mold Claire's positive drive—her aspiration for social position. Fawcett underscores the importance of heredity as a conditioning factor in the shaping of human behavior when he says of Slocumb, a minor character, that, "To speak more generally, the vast social momentum of heredity, which seems to be so plainly understood and so ill appreciated in our golden century, had Slocumb well in its stern grip."[39] As for Claire, she derived the gift of ambition from her mother's character:

But there was one more maternal imprint set deep within this girl's nature, not to be thinned or marred by any stress of events, and productive of a trait whose development for good or ill is the chief cause that her life has here been chronicled. The birthright was a perilous one; it was a heritage of discontent; its tendency was perpetual longings for better environment, for ampler share in the world's ·good gifts, for higher place in its esteem and stronger claim to its heed. But what in her mother had been ambition almost as crudely eager as a boorish elbow-thrust, was in Claire more decorous and interesting, like the push of a fragile yet determined hand through a sullen crowd.[40]

Her innate gentility, on the other hand, sprang from the cultivated bearing of her father's ancestry: "It may have been that the generations of gentlewomen from which, on her father's side, she had sprung, helped to nerve and steady her."[41] Claire's genteel bearing is so deeply ingrained that, when she enters the Bergemann household and finds herself surrounded by wealth for the first time in her life, she reacts as if she had been there before, as if this were her rightful place: "She was like a plant that has been borne back to its native soil and clime from some land where it has hitherto lived but as a dwarfed and partial growth; the foliage was expanding, the fibre was strengthening, the flowers were taking a warmer tint and a richer scent."[42]

The deterministic trinity is made complete with the inclusion of instinct as a guiding force. It is truly a three-in-one and one-in-three concept, for Fawcett does not present these powers as isolated currents but as interrelated influences. The fusion of instinctual response, hereditary marking, and environmental conditioning controls Claire's every movement throughout the novel. Her instinctive desires move her toward the city lights no less irresistibly than the moth is attracted to the flame. She is so much a child in the midst of force that the title of Theodore Dreiser's first chapter in *Sister Carrie*, published sixteen years later, could well serve as an apt description of Claire's uncontrollable impulses in *An Ambitious Woman*—"The Magnet Attracting—A Waif Amid Forces." In fact, Claire's fascination for the city is so markedly similar to Carrie Meeber's that the following passages from Fawcett's novel could be transferred to Dreiser's, and no one would be the wiser:

Claire fixed her eyes upon the shadowy city. A few early lights dotted its expanse with gold, as if to outspeed the tardier stars overhead. It spread away, for the gaze that watched it, like a huge realm of fascinating mystery.

The rapid darkness had thickened. Where New York had lain, dim as a mirage, hundreds of lights had clustered; their yellow galaxy more than rivalled the pale specks of fire now crowding with silent speed into the heavens domed so remotely above them.

But the whole effect of transformation, of magic, of mystery, and of beauty, which follows the advent of night along all the watery environs of our great metropolis, appealed to her with deep force.

Claire lifted her hand to her lips, and waved a kiss toward the glooming city.[43]

In *A Mild Barbarian* (1894),[44] published ten years after *An Ambitious Woman*, Fawcett shifts his Naturalistic perspective while maintaining his familiar format of initiation into New York society. This time Carroll Courtaine quits his rural setting, shortly after his mother's death. Unlike the pattern of many of Fawcett's other novels, however, Courtaine does not have to force his way into society; he is, in fact, courted by the elite because his uncle, Van Horne Courtaine, had been one of the wealthiest men in the country; and, in accordance with the terms of his will, Carroll Courtaine is to inherit one million dollars if he spends three months of the year, for three consecutive years, in New York City. Thus, when Courtaine arrives in New York, he is already the possessor of wealth and aristocratic lineage. He comes to know the virtues and short-comings of life in his new milieu during his three-year stay, and the novel concludes upon a note of conciliation when Courtaine, aware of the superficiality of his new life, but favorably impressed by the sophistication of his new friends, decides to reside permanently in New York.

Once again, the significance of the novel is not to be found in its examination of New York society. Fawcett merely utilizes the familiar background as the setting for the examination of a complex, profound, and topical question; for his real interest lies in probing the effect of environment upon human behavior. In other Fawcett novels, the protagonists had already been molded by their environment at the time of their first appearance; but, in *A Mild Barbarian*, Fawcett presents the struggle of the individual who is midway between the pull of two conflicting environments. The novel is less an assertion of the fact that environment shapes destiny than it is an experience that leads to the assertion. In a sense, the substance of *A Mild Barbarian* is the working out of the thesis rather than the predicating of it; its essence is conflict, not the charting of ineluctable deterministic movement.

Fawcett fashions Courtaine as the simple, unaffected, Words-worthian child of nature. His mother, who had reared him in the small, rural community of Southmeadow, had religiously protected him from contamination by any urban influences. There were only two sources of learning for Courtaine: he derived his lessons in morals and values directly from nature, and he became acquainted with the best the world had thought and said from Professor Dindorf, a scholar, who had rejected worldly values and settled in Southmeadow to live a life of quiet reflection and peaceful existence. The first section of the novel is steeped in natural description; and, as in *An Ambitious Woman*, the descriptive passages serve the twofold purpose of establishing setting and of suggesting the influence of environment upon character.

The novel opens with a description of the Courtaine house. The majestic simplicity of nature—and, by extension of Courtaine—is simply stated: "The road made a turn just where her plain old house rose from its modest acre or two of lawn, and soon she left off watching the gloom-dappled amethyst of the hills, and looked through a thick-boughed archway made by many towering roadside elms."[45] Nature's virginal essence and its deep mysteries per-

meate Courtaine's being every time the fresh evening wind, which
comes "straight from the dark hearts of the hills," blows in his face.
He is swept along by nature's vitality and is thrilled by its eternal
promise of hope and rebirth:

He passed a certain doorway and caught a breath of scent from its
pearly lilac-clusters. The next minute he heard the gurgle of a familiar
brook in a near meadow. Both odour and sound were part of the vernal hope and promise which this rising May moon made splendid
and sacred.
   At the professor's gate a large maple rustled its loose, ruffled leaves,
each green with that newborn balmy verdure which stays so brief
awhile.[46]

Courtaine, nurtured in this idyllic, pastoral womb, is the innocent, pure, ingenuous man, somewhat akin to Melville's Billy Budd
in his pristine beauty:

As he sat there before his old master and friend there was something
in his air and presence both childlike and yet wholly manly. A light,
soft beard clad his cheeks and chin with the effect of golden haze,
being so airy as not to hide their pure-cut curves. On his upper lip
the down was equally delicate, and if the sun had not tanned his skin
its fine blond texture would have been more apparent. . . . [His eyes]
were at once innocent, trustful, noble, and strangely human; a blend-
ing of grey and blue, usual enough as regarded their color, but oddly
and, to some people, almost oppressively earnest and sincere.[47]

These descriptions establish the purity of Courtaine's nature.
When the environmental switch takes place and he leaves Southmeadow "to meet the selfishness, the sorrow, the fretful turmoil of
ambition and greed" that characterize New York, Fawcett poses
two questions that occupy the happenings of the latter part of the
novel and form the basic intent of the work: does early environment
mold character so rigidly that it remains unaffected by all later
influences, and what is the consequence of the inevitable meeting
between innocence and experience?
   Courtaine does not slide easily into his new environment. His
innocence either offends his new friends or makes him the butt of
their sophisticated humor. He is ridiculed and scorned for commit-
ting such innocent offenses as speaking of learned matters and simple pleasures at dinner parties, where nothing more is wanted in

the way of conversation than the trivia of polite gossip. Society does not take readily to Courtaine, but he is sufficiently attracted by its wealth and glamor to discard the memory of his mother and the delights of his former existence at Southmeadow. He soon becomes a man bereft of the stability of abiding values: he is neither part of the new life nor possessor of the old; and, with nothing to sustain him, he founders between the two worlds. The similes of the novel stress the presence of the conflict. Courtaine may not be able to fuse the worlds of innocence and experience; but, ironically, the figures of speech in the novel do just that: "Carroll sat silent. A subtle bitterness had crept for him into the perfumed air of the room; it was like catching the scent of rotted leaves in a springtide walk through gayest greeneries."[48]

Courtaine cannot go home again, and he cannot make a home of his new life. Ultimately, however, in what emerges as the lamentable weakness of the novel, the combination of the two environments makes Courtaine the complete man. The lessons of his early years had made him sensitive to dishonest behavior and enabled him to reject the idle and dangerous notions of experience; and the worldly nature of his new society alters his naïve and humorless character, which innocence had molded, and instills in him the ability to appreciate the pleasures of urban civilization. Courtaine survives, for he synthesizes the best qualities of both worlds.

Fawcett began *A Mild Barbarian* with high purpose, but he ended by sacrificing the integrity of his subject matter to the demand of a happy ending. The artificial solution is lamentable, but it does not negate the profound substance of the novel itself—the environmental conflict between innocence and experience.

VIII *No Choice—No Morality*

The Naturalistic novel in which the actions of the characters are swept along a determined course to an inevitable set of occurrences gives rise, perforce, to an amoral thesis. If a character cannot freely create his own set of desired actions, if he can do this but not that, if he is deprived the dignity of alternative choice and is compelled to commit certain acts by the overriding pressures of internal and external force, then he can hardly be held responsible for the consequence of his deeds. Without a doctrine of responsibility, judgment fades, and acts become neither moral nor immoral; they are amoral, and they occur precisely because they *had* to occur, because they could not have transpired in any other way. It is as Fawcett writes of Captain Cummisky's ethical transgressions in *New York*: "He was the spawn of an evil code, a political civic grossness, which had nourished him from its poisoned paps and then reared him for the commission and perpetuation of its beloved misdeeds. His ignorance was the excuse of his vileness; he had been the pupil of blackguardism, not its master."[49] The code of corruption in city government had molded Cummisky's behavior, and so it, not Cummisky, is accountable for his action. The individual, though contemptible, is nothing more, therefore, than a blameless figure of pathetic helplessness.

In *Sister Carrie*, Dreiser offers an interesting insight into the dilemma of determinism and responsibility. He maintains that man, at present, is in the middle stage of his development, held somewhere between the beast of the jungle and the angel of heaven, caught between pure instinct and pure reason. Thus, Dreiser implies, to the extent that man acts instinctively, he is blameless; and, to the extent that he exerts reason, he is responsible for his actions. At this time in the history of man, however, the free will–instinct jangle is too confused to permit assessment of action; but, Dreiser concludes, man is moving away from the jungle to an elevation of reason; and, when he attains harmony of instinct and reason, he will take upon himself the burden of responsibility that comes with freedom of rational choice.

Fawcett's *The Confessions of Claud* (1887),[50] in the best tradition of the amoral Naturalistic novel, is an account of the torment experienced by an individual who is conscious of this human dilemma of action but who is unable to come to grips with it. Stylistically, the novel is reminiscent of *Ellen Story* and Fawcett's early experimental works. *The Confessions* is presented in diary form; the diary is written in the present by Otho Claud; but, since it wanders into the past and dwells upon past happenings, it permeates the atmosphere of the events with constant premonitions of impending doom. The tone thus takes on a Naturalistic suggestion as the sense of fate pervades from the outset: "Often on winter nights I have watched that rocky mass from the window of my little bedchamber, looming black and jagged against the brilliant stars. Child as I was, I soon realized it to be overhung with the doom of destruction. Slowly, like a devouring monster, I knew that the city crept every year closer to where we dwelt."[51]

This sense of disaster is always present. "How fateful those words of hers sound to me," Otho records of his mother's cautions, "echoing through the departed years! And for what a mournful reason have they found a lodging-place in my memory, ignorant as I then was of the disaster they foreshadowed!"[52] And the same note is struck when Otho tells his mother he will never forget the violence of his father's temper. The diary entry upon that occasion reads: " 'Be sure that you never do forget it,' she murmured, with an emphasis that I did not then dream of understanding. (How I was fated to understand hereafter!)"[53]

The novel proper is the confession of Otho Claud, whose father kills his mother in a fit of jealous rage and is subsequently hanged. Years later, after assuming a new identity and spending his youth in Europe, Otho returns to the United States, where Ada Gramercy agrees to marry him, even though he displays the same uncontrollable jealousy and raging temper that had destroyed his father. A rival suitor, Foulke Dorian, tells Ada of Otho's background; and Otho, fearful of losing Ada, kills Foulke. Ada advises Otho to deny his guilt; he does, is acquitted, marries Ada, and they live in relative happiness as Otho's will begins to overcome his raging, inherited temper.

Otho is aware that he has inherited the troubled darkness of rage from his father; and, throughout the novel, he speculates upon the condition of necessity:

This subject of heredity had just begun to fascinate me. But as yet I had scarcely given a thought to the marvellous phenomena of the will. The perception of how we seem to be so absolutely free and yet are shaped and moulded by the agencies of our environment; the recognition of how an immense sequence of mental conditions, from our birth to the actual present instant, precedes, like one long law of iron necessity, our existent state; the admission that any least or greatest act, from the mere lifting of a hand to the slaying of a fellow-creature, inflexibly follows a thousand previous acts, whether trivial or grave; —all this I had yet to ponder, to investigate, to accept.[54]

When Otho kills Dorian, he is prepared to absolve himself of any guilt by attributing the offense to his father's temperament, not to his own action: "It was with me as though I had ceased to be myself and had become my father! The man who had done that hideous thing years ago seemed to do it now again in my body, my spirit. It was the curse of heredity. I wrought the horror, as he had wrought it years ago. I repeated his act. With my brain mad, with my blood fire, I did what Leopold Clauss, who begot me, had done that day in the far past."[55]

The novel is not, however, an apology for human action. Vibrations of tension exist, for Otho is aware that the manifestation of a free will is an antidote to the helplessness of necessity:

To appear as the champion of a blind fatalism is far from my present aim. However pitilessly science may speak on this point—however exact and clear may be the deductions from certain undeniable data— however psychological proof may demonstrate that moral disease follows the same rigid law as physical, and that both can be transmitted from parent to child with an equal readiness—I am none the less willing to grant the existence, after birth, of vastly potent modifying forces. There are medicines for the soul no less than for the body. The world of philosophy and ethics, as that of surgery and pathology, teems with precious curative discoveries and resources.[56]

Fawcett does not attempt an intellectual resolution of the problem, and he concludes the novel on a Naturalistic note of ambiguity. The characters may speak of free will, but determinism prevails in action and outcome. The outcome itself is decidedly immoral, as Otho lies and wins his freedom; but with free will nonexistent, a rationalization is found for the murder, the lie discovers its justification, and immorality magically becomes amorality. "That is all," Otho concludes. "My story has been told. Many will judge me, should these memoirs ever be made public. But of all who read them who shall dare to say (whether his verdict prove harsh or merciful) that he has judged aright?"[57]

Clearly, one cannot judge the act; and, if this factor does not provide ambiguity enough, Fawcett teases the problem by having Otho and Ada live happily ever after, thereby suggesting that Otho can exert the necessary willpower to break the pattern. The reader is left pondering this perplexing middle stage of man's development (à la Dreiser), in which there is now a manifestation of free will, now an act of compulsion, and now an indication that the future is charted in the direction of greater free will. Otho Claud is, perhaps, best aware of the paradox—the necessity for the emergence of freedom:

I had been burdened from childhood with a curse, but no palliative was included in this fact. Untold advantages had been given me as weapons wherewith to fight against and conquer it. That I had struggled was no plea in my favor; I should have struggled with victory. . . . No; either my offence was rank and smelled to Heaven, or else all progress and reform, all evolution from beast to man, all rise from savage to humanitarian, all the mighty lesson taught by science, all the imperishable wisdom dug out of ignorance by dead and living thinkers—all was futility, sham, shadow! [58]

CHAPTER 6

Expatriatism, Fawcett, and the
International Theme

THE Realistic and Naturalistic elements in Fawcett's writings place him in the literary flow of his time, but other facets of his fiction, as well as occurrences in his own life, locate him within a wider current of expression peculiar to American fiction. The American expatriates and the international theme in American literature are complementary manifestations of this broader movement; and Fawcett's life and art brought him in contact with both.

American literature is not just literature that happens to be written by Americans. There are thematic concerns that distinguish this body of literature from other national expressions,[1] and the existence of an international theme is one such interest. The international theme is one of the earliest motifs in American *belles lettres*. It was implicit in Charles Brockden Brown's dedication of his novel, *Ormond*, in 1799, to a German friend. "My undertaking will . . . introduce you to scenes to which you have been hitherto a stranger," he wrote. "The modes of life, the influence of public events upon the character and happiness of individuals, in America, are new to you. The distinction of birth, the artificial degrees of esteem or contempt which connect themselves with different professions and ranks in your country are but little known to us."[2] The cultural contrast began with this assertion of cultural differences; it deepened as cultural ambivalences developed.

In his *Studies in Classic American Literature*, D. H. Lawrence insisted that Americans came to America "largely to get *away*— that most simple of motives. To get away. Away from what? In the long run, away from themselves. Away from everything . . . from the old authority of Europe, from kings and bishops and popes. And more." Lawrence argued, however, that the old master still

sits over in Europe "like a parent. Somewhere deep in every American heart lies a rebellion against the old parenthood of Europe.
Yet no American feels he has completely escaped its mastery."[3]
Lawrence explained the cultural conflict in terms of the American
psyche. But, whatever the compulsion, Americans have continually
looked back to contrast the manners, values, and morals of the
New and Old worlds, either to proclaim the success of the American
experiment or to lament its failure.

From this superimposition of one cultural pattern upon another
the international theme emerged. The theme is implicit in Philip
Freneau's *Pictures of Columbus* and also in Washington Irving's
A History of New York and "The Author's Account of Himself"
from *The Sketch Book*. It is also evident in passages from James
Fenimore Cooper's *Gleanings in Europe*, Ralph Waldo Emerson's
"American Scholar," and Walt Whitman's *Leaves of Grass*. Herman
Melville's *Benito Cereno* and Mark Twain's *Connecticut Yankee*
and *Innocents Abroad* are from the same pattern. But the theme
attained its ultimate expression in the novels of Henry James.

The American expatriate movement—the pilgrimage away from
these shores back to those of the older culture—is a nonfictional
manifestation of this fictional literary theme; and Edgar Fawcett
was as much a part of this movement as ever was Henry James,
Henry Adams, Edith Wharton, Gertrude Stein, or Ernest Hemingway. The motivation for leaving was seldom the same, but the fact
of their departure fused them into the same grouping. The artistic
necessity to draw upon the conditions of an established culture
propelled James; a society without form, other than the possible
emerging pattern of corruption, impelled Adams; Edith Wharton
fled from the stifling restrictions of New York wealth—her creative
fulfillment demanded a less narrow culture; for Gertrude Stein,
Paris was the center of artistic upheaval, of experimentation with
form in painting, literature, and music; and Hemingway, as
apocrypha would have it, went to Paris in search of Gertrude Stein,
and because the writers were there.

Edgar Fawcett became a part of the expatriate movement in
1897, when he emigrated to London, where he lived until his death
in 1904. Many factors prompted Fawcett to leave America, but he
never explicitly formulated any of them. He was not an Anglophile,
but he was of the opinion that the English soil had nourished the
greatest of writers—Swinburne and Tennyson among his contem-

poraries—and the appeal of living in the same environment fascinated him. Conditions of publication, which he felt were far more
favorable to the writer in England than in America, added to the
appeal. He held the abuses of New York society—the corruption of
wealth and political immorality—to be intolerable, and he sought
to remove himself from the unwholesome environment. And finally,
in leaving, Fawcett was rejecting the literary community that had,
by and large, rejected him. His writing, with few exceptions, had
never been greeted with enthusiasm; and he believed that the
venom of personal criticism had denied him his laurels. And so,
out of one part despondency—of never having been accepted; one
part despair—of ever being accepted; one part petulance—of refusing his talent to those who had hurt him; and one part hope—
of finding a more favorable literary environment and a more ap-
preciative audience—Fawcett joined the ranks of the émigrés.

There is still another reason—and a most important one—to
account for Fawcett's withdrawal to England and for the presence
of the international theme in his novels. His great admiration for
Henry James had left its mark. "Mr. Henry James' 'American' in
the Atlantic delights me," he wrote to Hayne on one occasion.
Other Fawcett letters reveal an extremely enthusiastic response
to James's artistry: "Henry James is now doing superb work for
the magazines. I believe that man will yet hold a place in our
letters equal to Thackeray"; "James's *Hawthorne* is a charming
book"; and "James's 'Private Life' story is I think exquisitely
written." In one letter, Fawcett indulged in a "hundred-years-
from-now speculation" and projected his judgment of James: "If
you & I ever meet 100 years from now, & clasp ghostly hands in
'No Man's Land,' I am sure that if we discuss the literary develop-
ments in a certain tiny, remote planet, we shall both agree that
H. J. *did* make his permanent mark there. Perhaps in a sepulchral
semi-tone I shall say 'I told you so.' "[4]

Fawcett never concealed his esteem for James's fiction, and the
impact of James's art upon him ultimately translated itself into his
own expression. William Dean Howells, in his review of Fawcett's
A Gentleman of Leisure, noted the influence of James upon Fawcett.
Though the review does not mention James by name, the allusion
is evident:

This is another instance of the international novel, the view of America

seen through eyes not alien, yet adjusted to a focus and perspective
different from our own. The author intimates this distinctly, and the
oppositeness of its aim and intent from some of those other stories of
similar construction; yet not only is the main idea, the position of the
hero, borrowed, but there are peculiarities of expression betraying an
influence which Mr. Fawcett would no doubt repudiate. One cannot
mistake the model of such sentences as these: "He had been from the
hour of his landing an admirable subject for impressions;" " 'Because
I must have taxed you so by asking you to do that little favor,' Mrs.
Vanderhoff returned, it deepening her handsome smile." [5]

The *New York Times* reviewer of the same novel did not hesitate to identify James as the influence. He even went so far as to
suggest Fawcett's mastery over James:

A short novel in the style of Henry James, Jr., but with strong distinctive characteristics of its own. . . . There is some clever dialogue,
and a good piece of wit is now and then introduced, superior to, in
its life, Henry James Jr., if not always equal to him in its fineness.
The characters are truer to the facts, but they want that intricacy
or that subtlety, which, it must be confessed, Mr. James somewhat
overdoes. They are in no respect psychological puzzles, but rather
the well-defined characters that are found in the modern realistic
drama. There is a minimum of plot and a maximum of dialogue and
description. [6]

The *Nation* reviewer of *An Ambitious Woman* called attention
to the similarities in the writings of the two men, and he also
compared Fawcett favorably with James. "So far as it goes," he
wrote, "it does something toward answering the question what a
high-minded American girl would do in a position of actual hazard,
with nothing but her own traditions to aid her. Daisy Miller never
had any traditions and the Lady of the Aroostock was so carefully
provided for (by the author) that no one ever knew what she
could do." [7]

Other critics, noting an identity of purpose between the two
novelists, rendered judgment in favor of James. The *New York
Times* reviewer of *Tinkling Cymbals* observed that "Mr. Fawcett's
favorite field of romance is one found in fashionable society. Mr.
James's inspirations are derived from pretty nearly the same source.
But the difference between these two writers is that Mr. Fawcett's
impressions seem as if they came from some one outside of this

particular existence, while Mr. James gives distinct impressions, not derivable from the outside, but from what the characters say." [8] Of consequence here is not whether Fawcett was the equal of James; he was not. It is evident, however, that his literary concern with the international theme ignited from a Jamesian spark, and the critics noted the parallels.

Thus the influence of Henry James accounted in part for Fawcett's involvement with the international theme. The pressures of cultural crosscurrents, however, were very much a part of Fawcett's entire life. They were in operation from his admiration of James to his removal to England; they were in motion from the infrequent international expressions in his early fiction to the developed manifestations of the theme in his last two works. In fact, the presence of the conflict colored almost all of his observations and shaped almost all of his views. It was at the root of his belief that American criticism was not so perceptive as English criticism; that American publishing conditions were not so advanced as the English system; that the American reading public was not nearly as discriminating as the English; and that American writers were unsophisticated fledglings in contrast to their English brothers.

Even Fawcett's own literary criticism was not something formulated apart from international considerations. His letters, which embody his critical opinion, reveal the influencing force of cultural considerations. There are no explicit statements within the letters that pronounce the inferiority of American literature or proclaim the superior nature of English writing, but evidences of this opinion are implicit throughout. His letters manifest the intensity of the conflicting national loyalties in his own life, and they uncover the depth of his involvement with the American literary formulation of the international theme.

It was not chance that Fawcett named two Englishmen as the greatest poets of his age. He believed the poetic spirit of the time to reside in England, and he maintained that both Swinburne and Tennyson had grasped that spirit. In fact, when Swinburne disappointed Fawcett and praised a republican spirit, Fawcett judged his view to be naïve. He lamented Swinburne's dim vision that prompted him to romanticize the virtues of America. "He quite over-rates our governmental advantages," Fawcett wrote; "his own country is surely *as well* ruled as ours." [9] Fawcett never overestimated the value of anything on the American scene. In the matter of literary taste, he held that it was a poor reflection upon this country " that so great a poet [as Swinburne] & one of so expansive a lyrical magnificence, should not have a better American constituency."[10]

Fawcett's remarks upon Tennyson are reminiscent of Henry James's reflections upon American culture in his essay on Nathaniel Hawthorne. Hawthorne was handicapped, James maintained, by the newness of his culture—by the lack of an American tradition to draw upon. In the same vein, but with a reverse perspective, Fawcett attributed Tennyson's genius to his inheritance of "English verse as Shelley, Keats, Wordsworth, Byron & Coleridge had left it."[11] He also alluded to the wealth of traditions and legends— the Arthurian legend in particular—that Tennyson had at his disposal to convert into poetic expression.

Most of Fawcett's praise for English literature was in tribute to its use of traditional form, its adherence to rules, and its concentration upon lyrical grace. On the American side of the Atlantic, how- ever, Fawcett saw a nation without the poetic inspiration of past times, whose writers were experimenting with innovation and re- flecting the present development of a new culture. Fawcett was on the side of the ancients; and, in his opinion, this American literature was a brash expression of an unruly people; he held it to be defiant in tone and unpleasing in form. His esthetic sensibilities were offended by the translation of a rude, democratic spirit into poetic expression. He insisted, for example, that Walt Whitman, the "con- tumacious buffalo of letters," was the archdefiler of the muse in America, the transgressor of poetic decorum. His reference to Whit- man in *A Gentleman of Leisure* was quite clearly contemptuous:

"What are his writings like?" inquired Wainwright.
"He calls them democratic chants. They are about boundless prairies and brotherly love and the grand coming amelioration of humanity. They are Carlyle and Emerson jumbled together in wild parody. He discards rhyme, he discards metre, he insults art. Of course he has a little worshipping constituency; such poseurs always do have. They think he is a mighty organ-voice. I wonder why everything that is rhapsodical, incoherent and bombastic is always compared to an oratorio or a church-organ. I advise you to avoid his book. It is printed at the author's expense; its name is 'Earth-Clods and Star- beams.' If that is to be the poetry of the future, Heaven have mercy on our unborn generations." [12]

Whitman's poetry reflected that part of America which was irrever-
ent of past European traditions, Fawcett insisted; it flouted the
laws of art; it sacrificed dignity for the preservation of the poet's
pose and the nation's barbaric image.

It is difficult to convey just how deeply Fawcett's views were
colored by cultural preferences and antagonisms, for it is apparent
that very few of his thoughts—and they were not all disparaging
of American accomplishment, as his novels reveal—were motivated
by more significant considerations. The international conflict permeated his entire existence; yet it was nowhere more manifest than
in his novels, which assume an important place in the development
of America's literary concern with the international theme.

I The International Novels

At times, there is only an occasional remark within a novel, such
as Miss Brown's idle comment in A Hopeless Case; but it is there:
"I think that the dowagers whom one meets are mostly charming.
. . . They make us remember that society here in America has
something solid about it. I should like, though, if we had titles here,
as they have abroad. Titles are so nice and dignified."[13] Then there
is the chance remark made by the Englishman about New York
women in Fabian Dimitry. Colonel Delamere comes to America
and observes that the ladies here are not yet ready for the titles
Miss Brown wishes to bestow upon them: " 'Pretty girls!' he grum-
bled. 'Yes; I saw a bevy of 'em just now—four or five, all slipping
along together like hoidens, and pushing each other with the
maddest screams. I've no doubt they were the sorts of American
girls who call themselves ladies.' "[14]

When Fawcett directed himself more fully to the cultural conflict, he usually reversed the traditional setting—the Englishman
was in America, or, more precisely, in New York. In New York,
Fawcett introduces Lord Brecknock and immediately involves him
with Grace Josseleyn, the daughter of an American millionaire.
Brecknock has lost his wealth, but he still possesses a title; and
he must maintain the appurtenances of that title—estates, servants,
costs of lavish entertainment. The Josselyns are eager to exchange
their money for the distinction of title and the attraction of culture.
In simple strokes, Fawcett presents the picture of the honest, bluff
American who has outstripped the Englishman in the accumulation

of wealth but who has never known the respectability of position and inherited nobility. The Englishman, on the other hand, only superficially bears the imprint of a desirable Old World culture; he must infuse it with a New World wealth in order to preserve and invigorate it. Both the Josselyns and Brecknock operate from an awareness of deficiency, and the marriage of the English aristocrat to the American heiress appears to be a union of mutual advantage. The Englishman, however, dictates from a position of strength—title is the more regarded attribute—and the Americans barter from a position of weakness, wealth is the lesser fortune.

The English-American contrast is not the major concern in *New York*; it was seventeen years earlier, in 1881, that Fawcett had first developed an entire novel around the international theme. In *A Gentleman of Leisure*, the Englishman makes his first appearance within the circle of New York society; but this "Englishman," Clinton Wainwright, is a young American, who, after spending twenty years in England, returns to these shores as a stranger. In a sense, he is the naïve observer who can contrast the manners, morals, and values of the two cultures without manifesting a conditioned bias for either. His inculcated values are offset by his affinity with the land of his birth.

During his three-month stay in America, Wainwright meets the stock characters associated with such a novel, and he draws the expected and appropriate conclusions. The Anglophiles make their appearance, and their affectations convey their disdain for American customs and their ignorance of English traditions. They antagonize Americans and Englishmen alike, and they thus alienate themselves from both cultures. As an American, Wainwright expresses his contempt for these men who reject the values of their own culture; as an Englishman, he betrays his amusement at their uninformed notions of English behavior.

The Anglophiles are a collective group in the novel, but there are also individual characters who represent distinct types. Bodenstein is the loathsome German whose combination of wealth (New World) and aristocratic mannerism (Old World) elevates him to the top rung of New York society. Wainwright, like Lawrence Rainsford in *Tinkling Cymbals*, finds this cultural synthesis incongruous and dangerous; he holds that the transplantation of social distinctions threatens the vitality of American republicanism. The Grosvenors, who represent the established wealth of America, are less attractive than Bodenstein. They, too, foster class differences; but, where Bodenstein displays a continental charm, they are austere, unimaginative, imitative, and without warmth.

Townsend Spring is the newly arrived American man of wealth. He is daring, speculative, adventurous, a man of riches today, poverty tomorrow, and riches again at some future time. He experiences life with great intensity, but he ignores the homely values of his existence in his obsession to accumulate wealth and buy prestige. His wife, who does not hesitate to trade respect for money, is crass and vulgar; her actions are immoral; her behavior, cheap. And, finally, there is Ruth Cheever, who is the forthright, sensitive, vibrant young American heroine. She is not overawed by the trappings of European culture, nor is she impressed by the splendors of established wealth or corrupted, as is her sister, Mrs. Townsend Spring, by the overnight accumulations of fortune. Clinton Wainwright marries her.

The novel suggests, as most international novels do, that there is good and bad in both cultures. In America, Wainwright

met quicker wit, prompter decision, less formality of intelligence, less needless deliberation and sobriety. It seemed to him that we drove at a livelier pace than they did in England, but that we avoided quite as many ruts and stones. As a people we fascinated him; he did not like what was coarse about us any better than he liked what was coarse about the country he had just left. Our inconsistencies often amused him as grotesque; our follies and foibles often wore him to a breakneck rashness; our very independence had sometimes a distressing braggadocio. He was perpetually wondering at our restless modes of living, our feverish tendency to annihilate time and to nullify space, our apparent constitutional feud with the idea of leisure.[15]

Wainwright's final decision to marry Ruth, settle in America, and run for Congress is a result of his having discovered American society to be more vital and more socially integrated than English. His presence in this country effects an international union of values —English cultural heritage plus American energy—that will contribute toward the creation of the ideal society.

Rutherford (1894)[16] is structured after the pattern of *A Gentleman of Leisure*. Duane Rutherford returns to New York after an absence of twelve years in Europe, and he is even more the naïve observer than Clinton Wainwright, for there is nothing American about him. His aunt, Mrs. Delancey, calls him an out-and-out foreigner; and a friend, Mrs. Calverly, berates him for his "settled convictions that all [his] country-people were vulgarians."[17] Rutherford's complete ignorance of American life is underscored when John Penrhyn, a rival for the love of Constance Calverly, tells him that he studied law in the West: " 'There are then facilities of that sort in the West?' asked Rutherford with a courteous surprise. He was about as ignorant regarding his own country as what we call a liberal European education is apt to make its recipients."[18]

Fawcett surrounds Rutherford with the usual gallery of "international" characters. The group begins with Stuyvesant, the Anglophile, who "was considered by many people excessively handsome; he had straight features, like his mother [Mrs. Calverly], and her mild eyes and delicate coloring; his blond beard and mustache were trimmed in exact accord with the prevalent English fashion of that special year; everything which he wore was, in fact, of the same contemporaneously English sort."[19] Stuyvesant's friends strike Rutherford as being English reproductions, "more or less neat according to the skill or awkardness of the counterfeiter, but rarely clever enough to run any chance of being thought genuine."[20] Mrs. Underclique, as the untutored, blunt but honest, independent American woman, provides the counterpoint to Stuyvesant: "Europe had pleased her, but it had made no decidedly favorable impression. She had openly yawned before certain grandeurs of art, but she had almost shouted with delight over others. All in all, she greatly preferred America to Europe, and told you so with unhesitating directness." [21]

Fawcett adds two extremely interesting characters to his collection: Philip Romaine, a poet in the tradition of Poe, who is convinced of the dominance of evil and darkness in the world, and Luke Paulding, a painter of wild murals, who functions as artistic counterpoint to Romaine. Romaine dislikes America; his antipathy, unlike Stuyvesant's, however, is no mere affectation, for it stems from his belief that America's obsession with goodness denies her a profundity of experience. He also holds that art emanates from tradition and culture, neither of which America possesses. To all effects, Romaine is an intellectual expatriate, who finds French culture more conducive to the creation of art than American: "He had indeed spent years in France, and passionately loved that country, disliking his own land to a degree which he was very candid about revealing."[22]

Paulding, on the other hand, is a painter with a Whitmanesque flair; his greatest desire is to paint the Rocky Mountains on the largest canvas the world has ever seen. What depresses Romaine about America excites Paulding; he is in love with its goodness, its innocence, its youth; and his paintings, though never successful, are attempts at evoking the wonders of America, the magnificence of the universe, and the awe of existence. Paulding's exuberance seems shallow beside Romaine's anguish, but Paulding is intensely alive whereas Romaine is cloaked in death.

It remains for Constance and Penrhyn to represent the best qualities of America; but, more than represent, they *are* the qualities. Their physical appearances, as well as their words and actions, depict the character of the nation. Rutherford looks at Constance and finds himself "looking with delight into the face that had been to him, since he first saw it, almost like a realized dream of chaste beauty, vigorous yet feminine, majestic yet soft, firm yet pliable. . . . How capable she looked . . . of consecrating every energy toward the attainment of some grand humane purpose."[23] And Penrhyn is nothing short of the rugged, innocent beauty of America itself:

He was of tall stature, of massive and sinewy build; perhaps his figure was just saved from clumsiness by its compact moulding; but he carried his head finely, like one who has assured himself, within the proper modest bounds, of just how much worth he is among men, and does not fear that his decision may undergo any injurious scrutiny. . . . True, he was unpicturesque; there was even a certain commonness about him . . . and yet there was no escaping the charm belonging to a frankly massive individuality not quite free from a peculiar gentle distrust of self, which seemed half to resemble innocence.[24]

A double vision of America emerges as Rutherford encounters the other characters of the novel. He finds the American desire to imitate European manners offensive, but the favorable impression that Penrhyn makes upon him alters his view of the new American. He loathes Stuyvesant, whom he sees as "the living representative of that pitiless idea, Caste, before which an old world had bowed for centuries, and to which our new world has paid devouter tribute than is always conceded"; but he is fascinated by Penrhyn, whom he envisions as the strangest possible combination "of the man and the child, of culture and non-culture, of dignity and humility, of grace and awkwardness. . . . I am truly beginning to think," he confesses, "that there are some very remarkable people in my native country."[25]

Rutherford's keen sense of judgment enables him to fit all the pieces together and to find a classification for each; but he can find no place for himself. He has been away from America too long to be a part of it; and, at the end, he becomes a wanderer, an exile, traveling between two worlds and experiencing the anguish of the man in the middle who belongs at neither end.

In *American Push* (1892),[26] Fawcett presents an interesting variation upon the international theme, a fresh set of contrasting pairs, and an altogether different perspective. The novel is about Alonzo Lispenard, a young American who loses his fortune and his fiancée, Kathleen Kennaird, in that order. Lispenard emigrates to Europe and becomes the art director of the kingdom for Clarimond of Saltravia. All goes well until Kathleen and her mother, traveling in Europe, arrive in Saltravia. King Clarimond falls in love with Kathleen; she, however, realizes that she is still in love with Lispenard. Clarimond gives her up to Lispenard; and, under the influence of the young American couple, he further liberalizes his kingdom by opposing his mother's desires to establish an absolute monarchy in Saltravia.

The American-European contrast is central to the novel. Mrs. Kennaird is the American pusher who married her English husband, Maitland, with the expectation that he would inherit his family's title and estates. He did not, and, some seventeen years later, still seeking the respectability of an English title, she almost forces Kathleen into a loveless marriage with Lord Egbert Dendudlow, a crippled English aristocrat. Lady Dendudlow, however, is made aware of Mrs. Kennaird's scheme, and she asks the American mother and daughter to leave her home: "Mrs. Kennaird's 'matrimonial plot' was soon on numberless lips. The society journals had their fling at her, and she was referred to as the 'inveigler' and again as the 'American pusher.'"[27] And so the two retreat to America, Mrs. Kennaird in disgrace and Kathleen in anticipation of her marriage to Lispenard.

Mrs. Kennaird is the ambitious, domineering, American mother of the novel. Her opposite number is Princess Brindisi, King Clari-

mond's mother, who is every bit as ambitious and unscrupulous
as Mrs. Kennaird. There is only one discernible difference between
the two women: Mrs. Kennaird fawns upon Europeans, but
Princess Brindisi can scarcely mask her contempt for Americans. In
a conversation with her son, Princess Brindisi reveals her feelings:

"If I were in any sense a great king"—began Clarimond with a laugh.
But the Princess stopped him, frowningly. "You're a very notable
and rich one," she said; "almost as rich as the Emperor himself."
"Well, granted."
"Almost as rich," she went on, with a bitter little laugh, "as an
American."
"Oh, they're not all so rich, by any means. And you hate them as
much as ever?"
"They are barbarians."[28]

Alonzo Lispenard is the protagonist, but his importance to the
action diminishes as the similarities between the family of royalty
and the family of "American push" become the main concern of
the novel. Clarimond's mother wishes to arrange a marriage for him
that will enlarge his sphere of power, just as Mrs. Kennaird wishes
to manipulate her daughter into marriage with a king. The aristocratic mother is motivated by the same desires as the American
mother; and both, in the novel's terms, are to be condemned for
their actions—one for desiring power, above all, for her son; the
other for desiring position, before love, for her daughter.
     The honest people are the two young children, Clarimond,
because he will not impose his authority upon others—he wants
people to react honestly to him—and Kathleen, because she reacts
honestly and does not allow desire for position to determine her
actions. Kathleen behaves as the ideal American in the presence of
royalty, respectful and nervous, but not obsequious. Clarimond
asks her if she is uncomfortable with him: " 'No', she answered.
'But mamma—oh, you *must* have noticed! You're a royalty, as they
call it, and you've turned her head. It's odd, too, for she has met all
sorts of great people—prime ministers, dukes, even the English
Prince himself. . . . I seem so vulgar when I talk like this! I do hope
you'll excuse me. No doubt you're used to embarrassing people,—
especially Americans.' " [29]
     Clarimond and Kathleen act as one: they both scorn the tradi-
tions and values of the past. In this sense, *American Push* does not

present the usual international contrast, in which the ideal is achieved by fusing the best qualities of the two cultures. The novel is more of a cataloguing of similarities than a contrasting of differences. The young people on both sides are allied against the destructive influence of their parents, and it is just this influence of the decadent past that they must overthrow.

The Vulgarians, published in 1903,[30] one year before Fawcett's death, takes an even more unusual approach to the international conflict than does *American Push*. Ostensibly, the novel has nothing to do with American-European cultural crosscurrents, but its concern with these vibrations is unmistakable. What Fawcett has, in fact, accomplished is the transfer of the international novel to the American scene.

Leander, Ernestine, and Lola Troop live a modest life in Stratton, California. They all move to New York City after their father's death leaves them with unexpected millions. In New York, they meet Marian Warrender, who assumes the task of civilizing the three young people and of acquainting them with the bored sophisticates of New York. Marian cultivates their manners, rearranges their values, and alters their speech. The novel carries the project to the point where Lola is polished enough to marry into New York Society, and Leander is disillusioned enough to return to Stratton to marry his uneducated sweetheart, Annie Shelton.

Fawcett manipulates West and East in the novel in much the same manner that he does New York and Europe in his other works: the West is to the East as the American East is to Europe. The Troops are honest, independent, unaffected people, but they react to New York personages with much the same deference and awe that New Yorkers manifest before European nobility. Lola, enamored of her new existence, takes on all the attributes of the older culture; Leander, on the other hand, is impressed by what he sees, but ultimately rejects it in favor of the untutored, pristine simplicity of the raw West.

Leander's action signifies the same resolution that Clinton Wainwright's does in *A Gentleman of Leisure* and, with even more pointed reference, Agnes Wolverton's in *A Hopeless Case*. He returns to the West with the learning of the East, and the new combination of manners and learning (East or Old World) plus independence and hardiness (West or New World) result, once again, in the ideal conditions for creating the best of all possible worlds. The American myth had it that the New World, located along the eastern seaboard, had been born out of the decay of western Europe. Fawcett was of the opinion that the passage of time in the nation's history had brought about a similar decay of the American East and had made the new West a fertile breeding ground for the spirit of American democracy.

II *The Last Manuscripts*

In one of Fawcett's last works, the manuscript of *An Innocent Anglomaniac*,[31] he returned to the foibles of the Anglophile, which had been of minor concern only in his earlier works. The entire plot of *An Innocent Anglomaniac* revolves about the foolish passions and misapprehensions of one of their number, Ernest Graydon, who is on a two-month vacation in England. In situation, then, the short novel is reminiscent of *A Gentleman of Leisure*, which places Clinton Wainwright in America for three months. All similarity, however, ends with this reversal of situation; for Wainwright is a mature, level-headed human being; and Graydon is a guileless fool, enamored of everything English. He is hardly the uncommitted observer.

Within days of his arrival in London, Graydon is duped by a confidence man, posing as a member of the nobility; he mistakes beggars for gentlemen, barmaids for ladies, and generally behaves like a country boy in the big city. He becomes ecstatic upon contact with English soil, and he believes he transcends the dullness of his American existence by breathing English air and sighting English clouds. The name of a barmaid, Miss Lyndhurst, conjures up images for him of abbeys, ruined monasteries, and ivy-mantled towers; and the most casual remark from an Englishman evokes from him the affected reverie, "how old-worldlike."

The work is not a serious treatment of the international theme, but a light spoof upon a limited aspect of the problem. The story is slight, but the satire is telling; and all ends happily when Graydon is rescued—with not a moment to spare—from the clutches of a blackguard who had preyed upon the innocence of the pitiable Anglophile. Graydon learns his lesson well and returns to America a more sober young man for his disillusionment. Fawcett does not contrast values in *An Innocent Anglomaniac,* but he ridicules an immoderate and foolish passion, born of a sense of inferiority and fed by a condition of ignorance.

In *The Pride of Intellect,* Fawcett's last major work before his death,[32] he manifests a more serious concern than he does in *An Innocent Anglomaniac* in reflecting the complexity of the cultural conflict. The work is again set in England, but this time, in a departure from his previous practice, it portrays Englishmen in England. Even within such a structure, however, the international contrasts are present. Two minor characters, Jack and Lizzie Prawle, brother and sister, are European travelers from Boston, Massachusetts. Jack is Ernest Graydon again, clothed in Sackville Street garb. Everything about him smacks of affectation, including his speech: "I say Lizzie," he admonishes his sister, "I've been hearin' your voice harf way across the drawin'-room. You'd better cut this rot of talkin' like a girl from the wild West. If you don't, I'm blessed if I'll not chuck the whole game and go over to Paris, leavin' you and the maid to shift for yourselves."[33]

Lizzie, on the other hand, is the antithesis of her brother. She has come to Europe in search of marriage—at present, a Lord Kilmerary is attentive to her—but she insists upon exaggerating her American mannerisms. The "wild West" speech reflects her national pride:

"Oh, *oh,* Mr. Indermaur . . . I'm just crazy about your splendid book! I've known exactly such women as your Adelaide. O'course she takes the cake for a nasty mean thing. You meant her to be a nasty mean thing, I'm dead sure, *didn't* you, now? There; that's right. Smirk; you've got such a beautiful smirk! I had a letter today from a friend across the big pond. She says everybody's reading 'Loaves 'n Fishes.' She went into the Big Store in New York the other day and saw a pile of 'em that looked for all the world like one of our skyscrapers. So I guess you'll have to come over and lecture. You can bet one thing—we'll give you a grand send-off in Bawston. There's no city in 'Merica where they love being lectured to so much as in Bawston."[34]

Lizzie's honesty and freshness make her much more vital and attractive than her brother.

The entrance of the Prawles in the novel permits Fawcett to satirize the English view of America. Whereas the American either cultivates the English manner or refuses to do so—both designs calculated to win approval—the Englishman remains himself. An English woman of fashion casually deprecates the value of everything American. In doing so, she reveals her own provinciality, but her reflections are her own; they have not been shaped by a desire to please or to antagonize Americans: "Algy and I took in Boston when we made our tour last year. It's a pretty fair town, with a largish green space at one end, which the inhabitants hold in great awe, but which isn't half so large as Clapham Common, though they never play cricket there, or anything like that, and are never tired of telling you that it's 'historic.' But we met some quite nice people in Boston. They have a curious style of speaking; one minute you find it like ours and the next minute you don't." [35]

The focus of the novel shifts from a contrast of manners to one of literary and cultural·standards. In rapid sequence, an American painter, Mr. Simonson, is introduced, offers pronouncements on literary taste, and then disappears from view. Before departing, however, he pleads for a serious acceptance of American literature, or, more precisely, for appreciation of serious American literature. With evident allusion to Twain, Poe, and Whitman, Simonson argues that the English welcome only the humorous, the fantastic, and the hysterical American literary expression, because they believe that "grotesqueness and caprice" reflect the idiosyncratic American nature. Simonson's plea, in effect, is for an acceptance of American literature as literature, not as cultural reflection; it is a plea for others to demand of it something more than a one-dimensional tintype of national life and to desire of it more than a barbaric utterance from an untutored people.

Implicit in Simonson's argument is the belief that American writing has not yet come of age and that the condescending attitude held toward American life by men of culture frustrates its maturation. Simonson's view is predicated upon the judgment that there is little or nothing of merit in the writings of Twain, Poe, and Whitman. The argument, since it is founded upon this unlikely premise, is somewhat forced, but it nevertheless stands as still another manifestation of the American desire for English acceptance so prevalent in Fawcett's international novels.

The international theme controls a fair amount of the action in the novel—possibly even more than has already been suggested. If Ralph Indermaur, the English novelist and protagonist of the work, can be viewed as an American—and this is not as unreasonable an interpretation as it might seem for there are many autobiographical implications in the novel—[36] then the cultural contrast becomes Fawcett's very personal focal point of the entire work. Indermaur, like Fawcett, is an outsider; he is not part of any group within the novel. The students at Oxford do not accept him, and the members of the aristocracy look with suspicion upon the upstart novelist. Indermaur's values, which are markedly different from those of the surrounding culture, are democratically inspired in his agitation against tradition and in his violations of the existing class structure. His virtues are typically American in a fictional sense: he is more resourceful than any of the others in the novel, more affected by matters of integrity, and more in possession of a sense of humor. Like many of Fawcett's other American characters, Indermaur takes pride in his own personal accomplishments; but he is also in awe of aristocratic personages. And, like the Josseleyns, Ernest Graydon, and Lizzie and Jack Prawle, Indermauer is willing to compromise or trade the virtues of his heritage for the privilege of winning acceptance from the English aristocracy.

Almost every attitude of Indermaur's had its prior conception in Fawcett's mind during his own lifetime, and it is thus not surprising to find that Fawcett's English protagonist is, in fact, an American character; it is but another manifestation of Fawcett's cultural confusion and another projection of his American identity. It is not surprising, either, that the manuscripts of Fawcett's last two works, *An Innocent Anglomaniac* and *The Pride of Intellect,* should concern themselves in part or in whole with the international theme. Fawcett lived the last seven years of his life as an exile in England, and the expression of the international conflict in his last works seems to be a natural consequence of his ambivalent cultural affections, which remained unresolved to the time of his death in 1904.

CHAPTER 7

Fawcett, The Critics and the Poetry

EDGAR Fawcett was a representative man of the latter part of the nineteenth century; for his novels reflected his life and times, and so did his poetry. Hardly an issue of a periodical appeared in the last two decades of the nineteenth century that did not contain at least one poem by Fawcett. He devoted a great deal of time to his poetry; and, by almost any comparative standard, his seven published collections alone would seem a significant enough literary contribution. The volume of the poetry pales in significance, however, when measured against the vast number of his published novels; yet the poetry earned Fawcett the higher praise. There were, of course, scattered unfavorable comments directed against it,[1] but the overwhelming judgment was that Fawcett was one of the better minor poets of his time, if not, as some critics suggested, one of the major poets of the century.

Fawcett, too, believed his poetic talents were of a higher order than his prosaic ones. "It is my own belief that my poetical faculty is my most authentic one," he averred in an article for *Lippincott's Monthly Magazine* in 1886:

When I am impelled to write a poem, there always appears to be but a single truly effective way of attaining this object, while in dealing with prose I am often more doubtful concerning methods, as if it were a dialect less natural to me than the metrical one. And here it may not be amiss for me to state frankly what I have tried to do as a writer of verse. I have avoided obscurity, aimed at a rich yet robust style, shunned mannerism, affectation, and mere dilettante archaism, striven to have my poetry reflect the time in which I live, cultivated with zeal the delightful possibilities of rhythm and melody, and cordially detested the prevailing impulse to employ sound as the inferior of sense.[2]

Fawcett's poetry did not always reflect a fulfillment of these grand desires, but it did gain him contemporary recognition. The *New York Times*, judging him by his best poems, not his most representative ones, ranked him high among the minor poets of the day;[3] it was also the opinion of the *Dial* that Fawcett's *Songs of Doubt and Dream* "fairly entitles him to a place among our American poets of the second rank."[4] *Harper's New Monthly Magazine*, which agreed with the judgment of the *Dial*, maintained that *Fantasy and Passion* was "a collection . . . from the pen of one of the most promising of our younger poets."[5] The *National Cyclopaedia of American Biography* was even more lavish in its praise: "in his verse there is that quality transcending talent, the individual and incommunicable quality of genius."[6]

Fawcett's poetry won its highest praise from other writers, and he valued these judgments even more than the favorable appraisals of the critics. Julian Hawthorne was one of his appreciators, and Fawcett luxuriated in this recognition. "What you write about my verses delighted and cheered me," he confessed in a letter to Hawthorne. "It is nothing to stir the shallow pools, for so many can do that. It is when we stir the deep ones that we are made happy; and to have given *you* a single real sensation of actual pleasure is an untold pride to me."[7]

Hawthorne derived a sense of pleasure from Fawcett's poetry, and James Russell Lowell responded to it with words of praise. Fawcett revealed Lowell's reaction in a letter to Hayne: "About Mr. Lowell: he is, I think, the only literary man to whom I ever addressed an unsolicited note. Some two years ago Mr. Howells took the trouble to write me that a poem of mine in the Atlantic called *Immortelles*, had won strong encomiums from Mr. Lowell and that he had asked a number of questions concerning me, 'very few of which,' said Mr. Howells, 'was I able to answer.'"[8] William Dean Howells, himself, in reviewing *Fantasy and Passion* for the *Atlantic Monthly*, said of Fawcett that, as a poet of Fancy, he "seems first among American poets." His entire review was in keeping with this sentiment: "The Fantasy and Passion of Mr. Fawcett is better named as to the Fantasy than as to the Passion. He is, to our thinking, eminently the poet of Fancy. In that he is a master, and seems first among American poets; we do not know why we should stop short of saying among all the English-writing poets of our time. Possibly Leigh Hunt alone surpasses him in our literature; we shall not try to establish his place too definitely, for criticism must not leave time with nothing to do."[9]

Howells's strong praise for Fawcett's poetry did not constitute a minority report. There were many such judgments. In fact, Richard Henry Stoddard, in *Poet's Homes*, devoted an entire chapter to Fawcett in praise of his poetic achievements. He offered his tribute without reservation:

But industry and versatility, only too often, as we know, accompany feebleness, or at least carelessness of composition. It is but justice to Mr. Fawcett to say that everything which he writes bears in a most striking degree the marks of thorough artistic care. A slip-shod rhyme, or an ill-constructed sentence are unknown amid his work. Not long ago he showed the writer a letter addressed to him by an eminent American poet, in which the following words occurred: "Whence come such intellectual power and constancy to your work, that you are able to compose novels, prose sketches, long poems and short, in so limited a period of time? And then the art of these pieces is always so admirable!"

Surely this is rare praise; but those most familiar with Mr. Fawcett's writings must admit it to be well-deserved.[10]

I *The Poetry*

The collection of poems in Fawcett's first volume of poetry, *Short Poems for Short People* (1872),[11] could hardly have been calculated to win critical acclaim. Certainly, no serious poet ever propelled his art into motion with so slender an output of innocuous patter and with so slight an evidence of poetic depth. Most of the poems are maudlin little pieces about death, God, and Sister Sue. There are, however, a few sprightly little verses that compare favorably with the general run of children's poetry, a "genre" that generally functions as if children were mindless little creatures, bereft of imagination. "A Sad Case" is one of the better poems in the collection:

> I can't understand why we don't like the things
> It's wholesome and proper to eat;
> I wish that I just hated candies and cakes,
> And cared for potatoes and meat.
> It frightens me sometimes, to think what I'd do,
> If only I had my own way

> In a candy-shop or a baker-shop,
>> With no one to watch me, some day.
> For if any one left me alone with a lot
>> Of candies and cakes at my side,
> I firmly believe I should eat, and should eat,
>> And should eat, and should eat, till I died.[12]

One other poem in the volume deserves mention. In "Above all Price," Fawcett enhances his subject by investing it with the melody of a ballad touch. The combination of song and simple sentiment makes it, by far, the best poem in the collection:

> How dear does mother hold
>> Her bonny little one?
> Just as dear as the jostling clovers
>> Hold the merry sun.
> How hard would mother try
>> To please her pretty lass?
> Just as hard as the pattering showers
>> Try to please the grass.
> How fair does mother think
>> The darling at her breast?
> Just as fair as the glad white sea-bird
>> Thinks the wave's white crest.
> How long will mother's love
>> For her treasure last?
> Just as long as her heart keeps beating,
>> Till her life be past.
> How much will mother's love
>> Change, as years are told?
> Just as much as the mountain changes,
>> Or the ocean old.[13]

Fawcett knew that poetry had the capacity to vivify the imagination of a child. That is, perhaps, why he began his career with the writing of children's poetry. He also believed, however, that great poetry was capable of stimulating the imagination of an entire culture into being and that, after all was said and done, the poem itself, and nothing else, was the glory of man. His own poetry matured sufficiently enough to enable him to express this idea in "Two Worlds":

A Fiery young world, in far voids of sky,
    Called to an old world growing dark and chill:
"Now that you hear the hour you must die,
    Tell me what mighty memories haunt you still!"

Then from the old sad world this answer fell:
    "Vast peoples rose and vanished where I swing....
But all my poor tired soul remembers well
    Are the great songs my poets used to sing!"[14]

II *The Dark Poems*

The great songs of literature might very well be those that take
man out of darkness into light, as "Two Worlds" suggests; but
Fawcett's understanding of poetic matter led him to proclaim that
the great songs of poetry celebrate the darkness as well as the light.
"Temptation" is a strongly dark poem, but it is very much in keeping with Fawcett's thesis:

Once, in the bleak gray bournes where ghosts abide,
    Nine spectral figures met, each gaunt and vast,
With blood-red lips, with faces hollow-eyed,
    With voices like a shivering autumn blast!

Then later to a poet whose cheek had grown
    Pale with the pain balked love so darkly wins,
They glided, saying in stealthy undertone:
    "Make us thy Muses . . . we are nine black sins!"[15]

In a letter to Hayne, Fawcett not only explained the poetic fascination he had for evil but also argued for its legitimate inclusion
within the province of poetry:

I have what are called peculiar theories, perhaps, regarding the
province of poetry. It seems to me that horror, duplicity, all human
baseness, may be included therein. I honestly don't profess at all
to know what poetry is. I know that certain lines, certain phrases,
thrill me, & that these are not necessarily yearnings after ideals,
longings for "the light that never was on sea or land," intense desires after inconceivable types of beauty. All these things *can be*
poetry, I admit, if treated properly; but the most revolting passions,
the most loathsome experiences, the most vile & cowardly & contemptible impulses, if dealt with after a certain fashion, if managed

after a certain sort of power & held in, so to speak, by a certain rein
—let us say the rein of genius—are also worthy of the sacred name.
Am I diseased? Perhaps yes. Surely my feelings, on these points,
are immensely unpopular. It is conventional to believe just the
opposite. Sometimes I wish that I could so believe. Mind you, I
worship color, sweetness, light, nobility of treatment, refinement of
aspiration—all these things are adorable to me—and *yet* I must admit
also, that one of Dore's most agonizing pictures—one of Swinburne's
most lascivious & outrageous poems—have force to thrill me after
much the same fashion as verse of artistic conception that brims
with the loveliest reaching after loftier life and supremer life-methods.
All this is a sort of confession.[16]

Good and evil are the conditions of man's existence, runs Fawcett's argument; therefore, evil is every bit as human as is good—
and it is more fascinating, too. The frightening depths of human
loneliness are much more appealing to the poetic sensitivity than
the upper regions of man's human strivings. In other words, Fawcett suggests that all human action and thought may be located
either on the well-lit surface of man's nature or within the infinitely
more appealing dark labyrinths of his soul. "Darkness" offers a
comment upon the inner anguish:

> I had a dream of a wild-lit place
> Where three dark spirits met face to face.
>
> One said: "I am darkest; I had birth
> In the central blackness of mid-earth."
>
> With a sneer one said, below his breath:
> "I am still more dark, for I am Death."
>
> But the third, with voice that bleaker pealed
> Than freezing wind on a houseless field,
>
> Cried, where he stood from the rest apart,
> "I am that darkness which fills man's heart
>
> "When it aches and yearns and burns for one
> It has loved as the meadow loves the sun!"
>
> Now I gazed on him from earth's mid-reach,
> And now on the spirit of death; and each,
>
> Though dark with a darkness to affright,
> Beside that third was a shape of light.[17]

There is something akin to Poe in all of this dark terror and fascination with man's anguish; but Fawcett, in another letter to Hayne, established what he believed to be his disassociation from Poe's esthetic theory:

I can't say that I agree with Poe in his definition of what poetry should be. It seems to me that poetry is not necessarily beauty of any sort. Beauty seems to us its most natural subject, because beauty yields most readily to the effects of its treatment. "In its ultimate essence," says Herbert Spencer, "nothing can be known." Heat, Light & Electricity are indefinible [*sic*] forces, and I do not see what prevents Poetry from being an equally indefinable one. We only know it by its *effects*. We recognize it in Milton's description of Satan & we perceive it in Tennyson's matchlessly pure pictures of Elaine. What we call poetry is really a kind of unexplainable transfiguring splendor thrown upon objects both material and ethereal. Pray, mark that word "transfiguring." Baudelaire has managed to throw this light upon objects of the most loathsome and noxious nature. The task of doing this is an *excessively difficult one*. To deal in the beautiful is much easier—possibly because of less inherent antagonism between the mode of treatment & its object. Surely there is much in what the world considers Poe's best poetry to be cast out of his works if his own definition holds good. Is not Tennyson's *Vision of Sin* a superb poem—and poetic in a grand sense? And yet it feasts upon horrors.[18]

Fawcett's quarrel with Poe is interesting, but specious, for it is predicated upon a misinterpretation of Poe's concept of Beauty. Indeed, Fawcett's Darkness and Poe's Beauty have much in common; they offer a penetration of man's soul and evoke a mood of somber melancholy. Upon occasion, however, as in the poem "Fire," Fawcett does leave Poe far behind in his desire to create the revolting, rather than the dark, passion:

> For all that lives I am a spirit of hate;
>   All beauty and strength I would annul or ban;
> And yet, through some imperious edict, fate
>   Puts my vast power within the rule of man.
>
> For me, to whom sad ruin and death are sweet,
>   This lowly slavery galls with pangs austere;
> I loathe the illumined hearth where loved ones meet,
>   The shivering outcast whose chilled frame I cheer.

> In the wide hurry and clash of this great town,
> I long perpetually, with zeal intense,
> To break the tyrannous bonds that bind me down
> And revel awhile in red magnificence!
> Thus with inevitable wrath I chafe and strain
> Amid my stern captivity's dreary days,
> Till after infinite effort I attain
> A riotous liberty, and madly blaze.
> Then in high watch-towers bells are tolled with might,
> And summoning peals ring loud above my roar,
> And bold men with my turbulent fury fight,
> Till, utterly quelled, I am a slave once more!
> But often amid defeat a thought that charms,
> While yet the water drowns my crackle and hiss,
> Is that I have wrapped some life in these wild arms,
> Or laid on some dead face my blackening kiss![19]

In such poems as "Fire," Fawcett more nearly approached what he felt to be the spirit of Baudelaire, rather than that of Poe. He considered Baudelaire to be "an excessively immoral poet" who cultivated a "diabolic fiendish style," and yet, he confessed, he was a "profound lover of Baudelaire." "Baudelaire . . . seems," Fawcett wrote to Hayne, "to denounce and *re*nounce all idea of virtue" in his attempts to transfigure the nature of the most loathsome and noxious objects.[20] Fawcett's sonnet to Baudelaire reveals his admiration for the "immoral poet" and his fascination with the poetry of revulsion:

> O Poet of such unique fantastic rhyme,
> Lover of some strange muse who bound her hair
> With poisonous myrtles, grown in no Greek air
> But fostered of some feverous Gothic clime;
> Degenerate god, half loathsome, half sublime,
> By what fatality were thou led to fare
> Through haunts that all corruption's colors wear,
> Through pestilent noisome paths of woe and crime?
> For me thy poesy's morbid splendors wake
> A thought of how, in close miasmatic gloom,
> Deep amid some toad-haunted humid brake
> That dark moss clothes or flexuous fern-leaves plume,
> Some rank red fungus, dappled like a snake,
> Spots the black dampness with its clammy bloom![21]

III *The Dark and the Light*

Fawcett's poems usually have an "either/or" quality about them. Either they are dark, or they are light; either song or story, fantasy or passion, romance or reverie. This separation of life into antitheses constitutes the greatest weakness of his poetry; it violates almost every insight into the nature of poetry from Samuel Taylor Coleridge's "Imagination ... reveals itself in the balance or reconciliation of opposites," to Shelley's "Poetry ... subdues to union ... all irreconcilable things," to Poe's "it [Poetry] is no mere appreciation of the Beauty before us—but a wild effort to reach the Beauty above," to T. S. Eliot's insistence upon an association of the sensibilities, to William Butler Yeats's summation, "Talent perceives differences, Genius unity." In Yeatsian terms, Fawcett was a talented poet; but he lacked the synthesizing faculty of poetic genius. In "Water-Lilies," however, notable because it is an exception, Fawcett attained the exalted vision of unity and composed one of his better poems:

> Up in the loftier leafage, dense and dim,
>> Of pines that slope to meet the lifeless pool,
> And with still spicy coverts clothe its rim,
>> The silvery fitful breeze comes fluting cool;
> But rarely does it steal to this grave spot,
> Dank with foul mire and rank with woody rot.
>
> From half-sunk logs the sluggish turtles peer,
>> The flabby emerald bull-frogs leap and
>> pause;
> The erratic dragon-flies float there and here,
>> With rosy flashes in their wings of gauze;
> And now a snake its sinuous way will thread,
> With flickering tongue and small dark lifted head.
>
> But out upon the central pool there blow
>> The lily-legions these dull waters hold,
> With hollowed petals dropping curves of snow
>> Back from the large fragrant stars of mossy
>> gold,
> All gleaming stainless on the unbroken sheen
> Of heart-shaped leaves, in blended bronze and green.

And as I watch them, in serene array,
  And muse, while scenting their delicious balm,
Of how they burst from soilure and decay
  In taintlessness of alabaster calm,
And blossoming from this grim half-stagnant lake,
What sweet pure incongruity they make,

I dream of gloomy souls within whose deeps
  Crawls many a cold uncanny reptile thought;
Where black hate lurks and torpid envy sleeps,
  And yet wherein some saving grace has wrought
Some heavenly touch that all their darkness dowers
With the chaste charm of these immaculate flowers![22]

IV *The Poet as Teacher—the Agnostic*

Much of Fawcett's poetry, be it good or bad, is a manifestation of working out of his esthetic theory; much of it is not. Writers generally regard prose as a medium for the expression of their intellectual ideas and poetry as a compressed art form for the revelation of mystery. Fawcett utilized his poetry and his prose for the declaration of his ideas; in fact, his agnostic beliefs shaped a considerable number of his poems. Robert G. Ingersoll, in his Prologue to Fawcett's *Agnosticism and Other Essays,* heralded him as a staunch foe of superstition:

Edgar Fawcett—a great poet, a metaphysician and logician—has been for years engaged in exploring that strange world wherein are supposed to be the springs of human action. He has sought for something back of motives, reasons, fancies, passions, prejudices, and the countless tides and tendencies that constitute the life of man.

He has found some of the limitations of man, and knows that beginning at that luminous centre called consciousness, a few short steps bring us to the prison wall where vision fails and all light dies. Beyond this wall the eternal darkness broods. This gloom is "the other world" of the supernaturalist. With him, real vision begins where the sight fails. He reverses the order of nature. Facts become illusions, and illusions the only realities. He believes that the cause of the image, the reality, is behind the mirror. [23]

Ingersoll called those who pierced beyond the veil supernatural-
ists; Fawcett identified them as preachers, ministers of God, and
keepers of the church. In "A Kind of Preacher," he castigates these
irrational, unscientific men of God; and, in the last stanza, he ridicules their smug certainty with a deft satiric thrust. The epigraph
of the poem records Herbert Spencer's observation that " 'Volumes
might be written on the impiety of the Pious' ":

A Mighty moral teacher this,
        Who deals, with finely flourished arms,
Now in damnation, now in bliss,
        Now sweetly comforts, now alarms;
And skilled to clothe each view intense
With pulpit-shaking eloquence!

Nothing too vague or too sublime
        Transcends his confident surmise;
The awful ambuscades of time
        Conceal no secrets from his eyes;
The deeps of space he coolly sounds;
He gives eternity its bounds!

On nature's plan his looks are bent
        And lo, she teems, we straightaway learn,
With special providences meant
        For his rare wisdom to discern.
He scorns what science may disclose,
For she but talks of what she knows.

Poor science, holding in her hand
        A few scant remnants of earth's youth,
And having at her slight command
        Nothing more potent than the truth! . . .
The sword of fact but ill appals
Where bigotry's great bludgeon falls!

He lifts aloft his pious gaze;
        In holy wrath his features glow;
For all dark sinning souls he prays;
        His congregation weeps below.
He sees destruction's giddy brink
Thronged with these rogues who dare to think!

But once beneath his throne we sat;
　　We heard his discourse, word for word;
And God was this, and God was that,
　　And God was thus and thus we heard;
Till we, who merely hope and plod,
Envied this bosom-friend of God![24]

In his prosaic argument, Fawcett contented himself with the
simple assertion that the existence of God can neither be proved
nor disproved. Ingersoll called attention to the reasonable tough-
ness of such a conclusion:

Mr. Fawcett has shown conclusively that it is no easier to establish
the existence of an infinitely wise and good being by the existence
of what we call "good" than to establish the existence of an infinitely
bad being by what we call "bad." . . .
No intelligent, honest man can read what Mr. Fawcett has written
and then say that he knows the origin and destiny of things—that
he knows whether an infinite Being exists or not, that he knows
whether the soul of man is or is not immortal.[25]

In his poetic assertion, however, Fawcett went beyond this measured reason. He upset the balance of his "can neither be proved nor
disproved" equation, by concentrating his attack solely upon the
dark gaze of the theists or provers and not upon the dim light of
the atheists or disprovers. In his poem, "In the Year Ten Thousand,"
he evokes a feeling of pathos for the ignorance of the theists as two
citizens of Manattia meet in the distant future and discuss the intellectual limitations of early man. Their colloquy, in part, centers
upon the confusion of God with Nature:

First Manattian

To think that in the earlier centuries
Men knew this planet swept about her sun,
And men had learned that myriad other globes
Likewise were sweeping round their myriad suns,
Yet dreamed not of the etheric force that makes
One might of motion rule the universe;
Or, if they dreamed of such hid force, were weak
To grasp it as are gnats to swim a sea.

Second Manattian

They dreamed of it; nay, more, if chronicles
Err not, they worshipped it and named it God.
We name it Nature and it worships us;
A monstrous difference![26]

It is clear that Fawcett did not believe it necessary to wait until
the year 10,000 for enlightenment; if man did not grasp the essence
of things in the present, it was not that science had failed man, but
that man, propelled by fear, had betrayed science by embracing
the superstition of theism. "Mr. Fawcett has shown that at the root
of religion lies the coiled serpent of fear," Ingersoll wrote, "and that
ceremony, prayer, and worship are ways and means to gain the
assistance or soften the heart of a supposed deity."[27] In "A Dialogue," Fawcett's Believer articulates this trauma of fear; but his
Infidel sweeps it aside and elevates the knowledge of life to the
altar of man's true god, his humanity:

Believer

This man of reason, whom you deem so great,
Who puts out Hell and bars up Heaven's fair gate,
Who flings all creeds terrestrial to one maw,
Huge as the Aztec battle-god's, called Law,—
Who makes the universe, to suit his wish,
As eyeless as a subterranean fish,—
Last night this valiant doubter, in his pride,
Shrieked for Jehova's pardon ere he died.

Infidel

With ease the partisan may falsely view
Delirium's rant; yet if indeed 'twere true
That some wild fear *did* seize him at the last,
What matters? Hardiest oaks are bowed by blast.
The warrior minds of men drink strength for strife
Not from death's opiate, but the elixir, life.
His life being great, who cares if near its close
He druled what imbecilities death chose?[28]

Fawcett's agnosticism was inspired by the times; but, more spe-
cifically, it was nourished by the intellectual leadership of two men,
who were also children of the same post-Darwinian-Freudian-

Marxian era. Robert Ingersoll was one of these scientific rationalists who carried the banner of truth and progress for Fawcett; Herbert Spencer was the other, and Fawcett honored him, as he did all his cultural idols, with a sonnet:

> A SPACIOUS-BRAINED arch-enemy of lies,
>> For years he has followed, with sure pace and fleet,
>> The stainless robe and radiant-sandalled feet
> That truth makes vaguely visible as she flies.
> For years he has searched, with undiscouraged eyes,
>> Deep at the roots of life, eager to meet
>> One law beneath whose sovereignty complete
> Each vast and fateful century dawns or dies!
>
> His intellect is a palace, on whose walls
>> Great rich historic frescoes may be seen,
>> And where, in matron dignity of mien,
> Meeting perpetually amid its halls
> Messages from victorious generals,
>> Calm Science walks, like some majestic queen![29]

V *The Tenement Poems*

When Fawcett freed his poetry of intellectual assertion from its confining dogma of freedom and its scientific rigidity, he frequently turned it to the same themes and subject matter that invigorated his novels. "Poverty," a social-protest poem, is reminiscent of his tenement novels, *New York* and *The Evil That Men Do*. The poem does not sprawl and dissipate its energy as the novels tend to do; instead, it combines detail with metaphor to create a Realistic picture of the city's poor and to magnify the horror of their existence:

> They that have borne such miseries yet endure;
>> They that so often have cried are crying still;
> We learn to name them lightly, these, our poor,
>> As part of earth's irreparable ill.
>> Us their sad voices have slight power to thrill.
>>> Their desolate haggard eyes but faintly grieve,
>>> Since we, who meet their anguish face to face,
>>> Through many a year its rigid truth receive
>>> As poverty's eternal commonplace!

All men, we muse, in shadow of trouble grope,
  Yet there are girt interchangeably from birth
With dubious gloom whereby the star of hope
    Shines vaguely on harsh crag or sinuous firth;
    Yet who may alter this unvarying dearth?
      Philosophy's astral splendors cannot light
        Cold want's disheartening dimness of eclipse,
      And science, although she weigh vast worlds in night,
        Brings no new morsel of bread to famished lips!

Famed thinkers, noble alike of brain and deed,
  Have grown white-haired in pondering how to give
These millions, bruised by poignant thorns of need,
    Some potent and benign alleviative.
    But still their burdening hardships grimly live;
      Still in the resonant city's careless heart,
        While deep groans pass on the wind like empty
          breath,
        Cadaverous throngs, mankind's far greater part,
          With rags for armor fight the assaults of death!

At toil they are stabbed with cold or scathed with heat;
  Tear-soaked, blood-stained, is the scant food they win;
From earliest youth round their unheeded feet
    Bloom tanglingly the red-flowered weeds of sin.
    Whatever bodily pain has worn them thin,
      Whatever sorrow has racked them, still they hear
        Starvation's rancorous wolves behind them press,
      While vice and ignorance, each with ghostly leer,
        Exult in mockery at their wretchedness.

Child after child, they are born to shame and woe,
  And stained at birth by even a mother's kiss,—
Too briefly pure, like those fair flakes of snow
    That fall amid the impure metropolis!
    What savage ineludible curse is this,
      O sovereignty that rulest fate and time?
        Why are these countless lives thus blindly wrecked,
      And made to dreary suffering or mad crime
        So terribly and so strangely pre-elect?

Age after age rolls onward; progress wheels
  Her golden chariot over shattered wrong;
Louder the limpid voice of liberty peals,
    Gladdening our world with archangelic song;
    Yet multitudes below the virulent thong

> Of this harsh doom go staggering to their graves
>   With feet that falter and with shapes that writhe.
> O freedom, poverty has her droves of slaves;
>   Thou holdest but humanity's mean tithe!
>
> They suffer and die; they starve, burn, freeze, and faint!
>   We hug our treasures, and the old ill endures. . . .
> How long, O infinite God, ere this wild plaint
>   Shall pierce the trance in which our spirit immures
>   Its best nobility, and the "mine" and "yours"
>   Clash with hate's fierce antithesis no more?
>   How long ere love on a loveless world shall flow?
>   How long, how long, ere we few, safe on shore,
>   Fling spars to drowning myriads there below?
>
> Have mercy, O men! O ye that strength possess,
>   Bridge firm, with pity and charity for span,
> The void of egotism, of selfishness,
>   Whose gulf so sternly sunders man from man!
>   Help with grand aid the unconsummated plan
>   Of centuries moving to millennial goals!
>   O seek that loftier grace, that richer good,
>   That prouder patriotism, where earthly souls
>   Meet mightily in sacred brotherhood![30]

In another tenement poem, "Nature in Bondage," Fawcett shifted his focus from the inhabitants of the city to the city itself. The poem extends the natural setting of "Water-Lilies" to the unnatural streets of the modern city. "Water-Lilies" locates beauty in the midst of slime and mud, but "Nature in Bondage" discovers traces of earth's natural grandeur alongside the stone, steel, and traffic of the city's streets. If progress diminishes life, the poem suggests, then nature, which is eternal and therefore admits of no progress in its static eloquence, must ultimately triumph over technology. It is not social protest that leads to salvation; man's moments of ecstasy reside in the spirit of natural wonder:

> I sometimes muse, in mournful way,
>   Since tyranny should make us mourn,
>   Of how the city's cruel sway
>   Chokes nature down with stony scorn;
>
> Of how, where traffic's noises rave,
>   Where dull roofs crowd and gray streets run,
>   The great primeval woods once gave
>   Their leafy laughters to the sun;

Of how, in purlieus wrought for ease
        And all that luxury enshrines,
Perchance a briery dell heard bees
        Boon dreamy round its eglantines;

Of how in slothful haunts of wrong,
        Where vice and squalor darkly merge,
Perchance a crystal brook's pure song
        Has thrilled the violet on its verge.

And yet, intolerant of thrall
        Whose rigid rule she may not quell,
I mark at many an interval,
        How fettered nature would rebel.

For clear in squares of courtyard space,
        Or breaks of foliage rarely seen,
Or grass-rimmed pavements, I can trace
        Her timorous episodes of green.

But where some fragrant park sweeps wide,
        Her woful slavery gleams more plain,
As though its captive yearnings cried,
        With lovelier eloquence of pain. . . .

Ah, Nature, find your comfort here,
        That still, for all man's power may do,
Your great heaven arches year by year,
        Its chaste unvanquishable blue.

And still, though art with garish light
        Your duskier mood dismays and mars,
Pale o'er the city, night by night,
        Beam your undominated stars![31]

VI *The Poet and the Dream*

Fawcett's tenement works railed against that afterbirth of progress: man's degradation. They exposed the brutal existence of New York's working population. The other side of New York life, however, held greater fascination for Fawcett. A significant number of his novels swirled within the rarefied air breathed by New York's aristocracy. Fawcett chastised the aristocrats for indulging themselves in sterile and incestuous interchange, far removed from the madding crowd, and, more importantly, for perverting the American ideal of democratic equality.

The poem "The Bartholdi Statue (Unveiled on Bedloe's Island, October 28, 1886)" is akin to Fawcett's society novels in that it records the failure of the American Dream, its emergence into the terror of nightmare, and yet the promise of its fulfillment. The poem is *Tinkling Cymbals* and Lawrence Rainsford all over again; it is in the spirit of Jonathan Woolman[32] and his prophecy of ruin, of Emerson and his assertion of American necessity in the "American Scholar" address, and of Whitman and his projection of hope in *Democratic Vistas*. The Statue in the poem speaks:

> Here is my boon, ye people I would test.
> Heed that ye use it well; the choice is yours.
> Much have ye done, yet much remains to do
> Ye fought with foes o'erseas until ye tore
> This coign of continent from tyranny,
> Standing thenceforth sublime in solitude
> Among all nations. Yet ye have not kept
> Promise with your ideal, and threat to lapse
> From the white summit of its dignities
> More than ye grant this hour. Democracy
> Is louder on your lips than in your deeds.
> The few grow sleek with gains that make their vaults
> Harbors of futile treasure; one throng sweats
> For bread to breathe by; one, still vaster, bows
> In yokes of toil that drag it nigh the brute.
>
> . . . .
>
>   Crowd your schools
> With learning and sweet discipline of chiefs
> Versed in all wise experience, till their lore
> Make Athens of your slums, and parents loth
> To let their children drink at such pure streams,
> Common as they are pure, be scathed with scorn.
> Abase the vaunts of caste; your earls and dukes
> Can win their earldoms and their dukedoms best
> By that sole patent of nobility
> A blameless manhood may confer on them,
> Not by the coronets and strawberry-leaves
> Dead kings have flung their bastards. Hold your arts
> In reverence, and revering shield their rights,
> Till he who tells with chisel, brush or plume
> Your annals, may not starve at such high task;
> For poet, novelist, painter, sculptor, stands
> Each as a firm caryatid that shall grace
> The pediment of your unborn renown![33]

CHAPTER *8*

Conclusion

I T is ironic that our study of literature has become fragmentary when literature is an art that reveals itself in putting pieces together, in ordering environment, in shaping the happenstance of experience, in synthesizing irreconcilable facets of existence, and in imposing form upon formlessness, order upon chaos. Students of literature have come to think in terms of classification: classification by period; classification by genre—and here by subclassifications, the short story, the short short story, the long short story, the novella, and the novelette—classification by school, Expressionist, Absurdist, Naturalist, Realist, and on ad infinitum; and classification by author.

In the study of late nineteenth-century American literature, we turn to Emily Dickinson for a taste of poetry; to James Herne and Bronson Howard for an understanding of drama; to Henry James for a view of the international novel; to Frances Hodgson Burnett for a glimpse into the fiction of romance; to William Dean Howells for an insight into Realism; to Jack London, Stephen Crane, or Frank Norris for an illumination of Naturalism; to Theodore Dreiser for a revelation of the American Dream; and to Henry Adams or Mark Twain for an awareness of skepticism. These literary expressions in isolation underscore the value and contribution of Edgar Fawcett, for he was a writer who did it all; that accomplishment is precisely the mark and the significance of the representative author.

The latter quarter of the nineteenth century was a complex era. It was Henry Adams's age of multiplicity; and Edgar Fawcett, though not a great writer, was the multiple man of his time, the representative man at the twilight of the century. He was a writer of romance during the decline of the romantic novel and a Realistic writer upon the emergence of literary Realism; he was a Naturalist, whose novels were shaped by a current of deterministic thought and an agnostic in an age of skepticism; he was a critic of American capitalism during a period of consolidation of wealth, a spokesman for the impoverished at a time of industrial exploitation, and a projector of the American Dream in the finest tradition of American letters. Idealist though he was, Fawcett ultimately became disillusioned with America and emigrated to England; he thus became a part of the expatriate movement also; and his writing reflected the international dilemmas of that movement.

Henry Steele Commager, in *The American Mind*, theorizes that the most important decade in American history began to unfold in the year 1890. An understanding of the last ten years of that century, he maintains, is crucial to an understanding of the present. It is evident that the study of a representative man would provide a key into the complexities of the time; and Edgar Fawcett, despite his present literary obscurity, is that representative man. A study of the nineteenth century would be less than complete without him, for Edgar Fawcett's life and writings *are* the life and writings of the close of that century.

Notes and References

Preface

1. Crane Brinton, *The Political Ideas of the English Romanticists* (England, 1926), pp. 5–6.

2. George Parsons Lathrop, "The Literary Movement in New York," *Harper's New Monthly Magazine* (November, 1886), 819. The *Scribner* review of Fawcett's *Fantasy and Passion*, June, 1878, also notes that "he [Fawcett] has, probably, printed a greater number of verses during the last ten years than any other writer in America."

3. William H. Rideing, "Edgar Fawcett," *Bookman*, XXXII (December, 1910), 436.

4. The numbers given for publications and dramatic productions are reasonably, but not absolutely, accurate. The occasional difficulty in distinguishing between a novel and a short story accounts, in part, for the speculative nature of the figures, and the problems in verifying dramatic productions create further confusion.

5. William Dean Howells, *Atlantic Monthly*, XLI (May, 1878), 632. For a fuller account of Howells's statement, see pp. 93–94.

6. Aldrich and Fawcett were good friends; Whittier, on a number of occasions, spoke favorably of Fawcett's poetry; Lowell thought Fawcett's "Immortelles" to be a good poem (see p. 93); Hamlin Garland sought Fawcett's literary opinions; Oscar Wilde stayed at Fawcett's house while in New York; and Henry James thought enough of Fawcett to send him copies of his novels. The opinion these men held of Fawcett is revealed in Fawcett's letters. For their comment and for fuller reference to other Fawcett letters mentioned in this study, see my edition of Fawcett's letters, "Through a Nineteenth-Century Looking Glass: The Letters of Edgar Fawcett," *Tulane Studies in English*, XV (1967), 107–57.

Chapter One

1. There is even less information of Fawcett's early years in *Who's Who in America*, *Appleton's Cyclopaedia of American Biography*, *American Authors and Books*, and *The National Cyclopaedia of American Biography*.

2. *Dictionary of American Biography* (New York, 1931), VI, 302.
3. *New York Times,* June 22, p. 4.
4. Fawcett letter to Paul Hamilton Hayne, July 19, 1876. All letters to Hayne courtesy the Duke University Library.
5. *Ibid.,* February 6, 1878, and July 14, 1878.
6. *Ibid.,* July 28, 1876.
7. *Ibid.,* September 17, 1878.
8. *Ibid.,* December 19, 1878.
9. William H. Rideing, "Edgar Fawcett," *Bookman,* XXXII (December, 1910), 436–39.
10. "A Few Literary Experiences," *Lippincott's Monthly Magazine,* XXXVII (1886), 412–14.
11. The dates of these letters are: May 10, 1875; August 8, 1876; n.d., 1876; and December 19, 1878.
12. Fawcett expresses the same sentiment and makes use of the same phrase in his novel, *The Pride of Intellect.* For publishing information and a speculation upon the date of the novel, see Chapter 1, fn. 14.
13. Fawcett letters to Edmund Clarence Stedman, July 22, 1889, and August 15, 1889. Excerpts from these letters are printed courtesy the Columbia University Library.
14. The manuscript of *The Pride of Intellect* was found by Mr. and Mrs. William Murney in a carton on the de Coppet estate in Narragansett, Rhode Island. The de Coppets, two unmarried sisters, were Fawcett's nieces. The manuscript is legibly written in Fawcett's own hand, his signature appears on the first and last page, and his address—7 St. Loo Mansions, Cheyne Gardens, Chelsea, S.W., London—appears on the first page. Since the *Dictionary of American Biography* locates Fawcett's address at death in the Chelsea district of London, and since his previous London addresses from 1899 to 1903, as listed in *Who's Who in America,* were not in the Chelsea area, it seems reasonable to assume that Fawcett began and completed the novel while he lived in Chelsea, which would have been early in 1904. Shortly before his death, Fawcett either mailed the manuscript to his nieces in Narragansett for possible American publication, or, more likely, someone else sent his effects to the de Coppet sisters after his death in 1904. For the only printed text of the novel, see my Ph.D. dissertation, "Edgar Fawcett, A Minor Writer in the Literary Current of His Time: an Edition of His Unpublished Novel, *The Pride of Intellect,*" Michigan State University, 1964.
15. *Ibid.,* pp. 210–12.
16. Fawcett letter to Hayne, September 24, 1876.
17. Frank Luther Mott, *Golden Multitudes* (New York, 1947), pp. 148–55.

18. Fawcett letter to Bayard Taylor, March 3, 1878, printed courtesy the Cornell University Library.

19. Fawcett letter to Dana (no last name), an editor, printed courtesy the University of Virginia Library.

20. Fawcett letter to publisher, Mr. Paine, November 21; the year is probably 1897, as Fawcett and Paine corresponded prior to the publication of Fawcett's novel, *New York,* in 1898. All letters to Paine are printed courtesy the Henry E. Huntington Library and Art Gallery.

21. Fawcett letter to Hayne, October 10, 1877.

22. Fawcett letter to Paine, probably 1898; see Chapter 1, fn. 20.

23. Jeanette Gilder, "The Lounger," *Critic* (February 15, 1896), p. 114.

24. Hellmut Lehmann-Haupt, *The Book in America* (New York, 1952), p. 114.

25. *Agnosticism and Other Essays* (New York, 1889), p. 35.

26. *Ibid.,* p. 62.

27. "To Robert G. Ingersoll," *Arena,* IX (December, 1893), p. 117.

28. "The Woes of the New York Working-Girl," *Arena,* V (December 1891), 34.

29. "Plutocracy and Snobbery in New York," *Arena,* IV (July, 1891), 151.

30. Fawcett letter to "Dear Sir," October 18, no year, printed courtesy the State University of New York at Buffalo Library.

31. Fawcett letter to Hayne, n.d., 1876.

32. Fawcett letter to Hayne, November 19, 1876.

33. Fawcett letter to Hayne, March 14, 1876.

34. The poet and critic is R. H. Stoddard. Fawcett relates the same story in a letter to Hayne, February 6, 1878.

35. "Should Critics Be Gentlemen?," *Lippincott's Monthly Magazine,* XXXIX (1887) 163–67.

Chapter Two

1. I have gathered the critical comment on Fawcett and his works from one newspaper, the *New York Times,* and nine periodicals: the *Atlantic Monthly,* the *Bookman,* the *Catholic World,* the *Critic,* the *Dial, Harper's New Monthly Magazine,* the *Independent, Lippincott's Monthly Magazine,* and the *Nation.* The list of these periodicals is, of necessity, selective, inasmuch as there were some 2,400 periodicals in existence in 1880, about 3,300 in 1885, and 4,400 by 1890. With the exceptions of the *Catholic World,* the *Independent,* and the *New York Times,* the magazines I utilized were the ones Fawcett had

published in, those he commented upon in his letters, and those that
had attained a responsible literary reputation. The review printed
from the *Catholic World* is included because it is both perceptive and
typical in its expression; the *Independent* review is a strong expression of a rather common anti-Realistic literary point of view; and since
most of Fawcett's works are set in New York City, the newspaper
reaction of the *New York Times,* which reflects a popular literary
opinion, is very much to the point. Frank Luther Mott discusses the
literary importance of the other periodicals in volumes 3 and 4 of
his *A History of American Magazines* (Cambridge, 1938 and 1957):

> *Lippincott's* . . . must be given a high rank among American
> magazines (v. 3, p. 401).
> Perhaps there was a more consistent excellence in the book re-
> views of the *Nation,* the *Critic,* the *Dial,* and the *Atlantic* than
> in those of other periodicals (v. 3, p. 232).
> The most important journals of this period devoted to criticism
> of current literature were . . . the *Critic* . . . the *Dial* . . . [and]
> Harry Thurston Peck's *Bookman* . . . (v. 4, p. 124).
> At the beginning of the twenty-year period 1885-1905, the lead-
> ers in the field of national illustrated monthlies devoted to the
> publication of literary miscellany were two New York magazines,
> *Harper's* and the *Century* (v. 4, p. 43).
> The *Atlantic Monthly* of Boston occupied, in the words of the
> *Dial,* "a place by itself." And that old-school critic went on to
> say that the *Atlantic* stood "more distinctly for culture than any
> other American magazine" (v. 4, p. 44).

2. Hamlin Garland also objected to the artificially contrived plot
of *Miriam Balestier.* In a letter to Garland, dated November 6, 1888,
Fawcett wrote: "I was very glad to get your exceedingly kind note.
I agree with all your less eulogistic words about my poor little story.
The railway accident *is* perhaps a *deus ex,* though I somehow didn't
want it to be just that. I, too, hate the 'happening' of things in a
novel. At the same time, I believe firmly in coincidences, and although the entire human story often seems to me ragged, contradic-
tory, plotless, indeterminate, still I should be inclined to insist on
occasional 'touches' in it just like that of the train tumbling over an
embankment at the precise instant of Paula's meditated crime. However, I am not defending myself."

The excerpt from this letter is printed courtesy the University of
Southern California Library.

3. Review of *Miriam Balestier, Critic,* XI (March 23, 1889),
142–43.

4. Review of *The Adventures of a Widow, Nation,* XXXIX (October 9, 1884), 314.

5. Review of *A Demoralizing Marriage, Critic,* XI (April 6, 1889), 167.

6. Review of *Social Silhouettes, Athenaeum,* reprinted in the *Critic,* V (January 23, 1886), 48.

7. Review of *The House at High Bridge, Dial,* VII (December, 1886), 189–90.

8. Review of *A Mild Barbarian, New York Times* (October 14, 1894), 27.

9. Review of *A Hopeless Case, New York Times* (June 27, 1880), p. 10.

10. Review of *An Ambitious Woman, New York Times* (December 17, 1883), p. 3.

11. Fawcett letter to Hayne, 1876.

12. Fawcett letter to Hayne, February 2, 1879.

13. Review of *A Hopeless Case, Atlantic Monthly,* XLVI (September, 1880), 415–16.

14. Review of *A Man's Will, Nation,* XLVI (June 28, 1888), 530.

15. Review of *Tinkling Cymbals, New York Times* (June 22, 1884), p. 5.

16. Review of *Tinkling Cymbals, Nation,* XXXIX (July 31, 1884), 96.

17. See Chapter 2, fn. 6.

18. Review of *Rutherford, New York Times* (August 23, 1884), p. 3.

19. Fawcett letter to Hayne, n.d., 1876.

20. Review of *A New York Family, Catholic World,* LV (July, 1892), 599–600.

21. Review of *An Ambitious Woman, Atlantic Monthly,* LIII (May 1884), 711.

22. Review of *An Ambitious Woman, New York Times* (December 17, 1883), 3.

Chapter Three

1. *Divided Lives,* Chicago, 1888.

2. *Miriam Balestier,* Chicago, 1888.

3. *Olivia Delaplaine,* Boston, 1888.

4. *Ibid.,* p. 340.

5. *How a Husband Forgave,* New York, 1890.

6. *A Daughter of Silence,* New York, 1890.

7. *Women Must Weep,* Chicago, 1891.

8. *Ibid.*, p. 45.

9. *Loaded Dice*, New York, 1891.

10. *The Adopted Daughter*, Chicago, 1892.

11. *Her Fair Fame*, New York, 1894.

12. *A Romance of Old New York*, Philadelphia, 1897.

13. *Solarion*, Philadelphia, 1889.

14. *The New Nero*, New York, 1893.

15. *The Ghost of Guy Thyrle*, New York, 1896.

Chapter Four

1. For a brief account of this controversy, see Mott's *History of American Magazines*, vol. 4, pp. 111–13 and 121–24.

2. George Pellow, "The New Battle of the Books," *Forum* (July, 1888), 564.

3. Nancy Banks, "Two Recent Revivals in Realism," *Bookman* (June, 1899), 356–57.

4. Anon., *Belford's Magazine* (July, 1888), p. 263.

5. Amelia Barr, "The Modern Novel," *North American Review* (November, 1894), p. 598.

6. William Dean Howells, "Criticism and Fiction," *Criticism and Fiction and Other Essays*, eds. Clara and Rudolf Kirk (New York, 1959), pp. 15 and 17.

7. Review of *Tinkling Cymbals, New York Times,* (June 22, 1884), p. 5.

8. Review of *New York, New York Times* (October 8, 1898), p. 662.

9. Anon., "Chronicle and Comment," *Bookman* (June, 1904), pp. 341–42.

10. Review of *New York, New York Times* (January 28, 1899), p. 64.

11. Review of *A Man's Will, New York Times* (July 22, 1888), p. 10.

12. Review of *A Man's Will, Nation*, XLVI (June 28, 1888) 530.

13. Review of *A Gentleman of Leisure, New York Times* (July 10, 1881), p. 10.

14. Review of *Ellen Story, Harper's New Monthly Magazine*, LIII (1876), 629.

15. Review of *A New York Family, Critic*, XV (June 27, 1891), 335.

16. Review of *Purple and Fine Linen, Nation*, XVII (July 10, 1873), 27.

17. Review of *Tinkling Cymbals, Lippincott's Monthly Magazine* (August, 1884), p. 215.
18. Review of *New York, Independent*, LI (January 26, 1899), 280.

Chapter Five

1. Fawcett's letters to the young Garland offer him courage and literary advice. For Fawcett's half of the correspondence, see my edition of Fawcett's letters in *Tulane Studies in English*.
2. There is no extant edition of Fawcett's first published novel, *Asses Ears* (New York, 1871).
3. *Purple and Fine Linen*, New York, 1873.
4. *A Hopeless Case*, Boston, 1880.
5. *Ibid.*, pp. 253–54.
6. *Ibid.*, pp. 249–50.
7. *The Adventures of a Widow*, Boston, 1884
8. *Ibid.*, p. 282.
9. *Tinkling Cymbals*, Boston, 1884.
10. *Ibid.*, pp. 254–56.
11. *Ibid.*, pp. 263–64.
12. *Ibid.*, p. 13.
13. *Ibid.*, p. 123.
14. *Ibid.*, p. 325
15. *Ellen Story*, New York, 1876.
16. *Ibid.*, p. 21.
17. *Ibid.*, pp. 79–80.
18. This idea of collapsing time is what modern literature and T. S. Eliot's mythic method is all about. In his review of James Joyce's *Ulysses*, Eliot called attention to Joyce's technique of fusing antiquity with contemporaneity, and he hailed the work as making the modern world possible for art.
19. *A Man's Will*, New York, 1888.
20. *Ibid.*, pp. 278–79.
21. *A New York Family*, New York, 1891.
22. *New York*, New York, 1898.
23. For excerpts from the reviews, see pp. 36–39.
24. *New York*, pp. 31–32.
25. *The Evil That Men Do*, New York, 1889.
26. *The House at High Bridge* (Boston, 1887), p. 245.
27. Henry Steele Commager, *The American Mind* (New Haven, 1950), p. 108.
28. *A Demoralizing Marriage*, Philadelphia, 1889.
29. *Ibid.*, p. 63.

30. *Ibid.*, p. 178.
31. *Ibid.*, pp. 180–81.
32. *Outrageous Fortune,* New York, 1894.
33. *Ibid.*, p. 327.
34. *Ibid.*, pp. 30–31.
35. *Ibid.*, p. 316.
36. *New York,* pp. 30–31.
37. *An Ambitious Woman,* Boston, 1884.
38. *Ibid.*, p. 52.
39. *Ibid.*, p. 101.
40. *Ibid.*, p. 8.
41. *Ibid.*, p. 43.
42. *Ibid.*, pp. 145–46.
43. *Ibid.*, pp. 69, 77, 81, and 71.
44. *A Mild Barbarian,* New York, 1894.
45. *Ibid.*, pp. 1–2.
46. *Ibid.*, p. 5.
47. *Ibid.*, pp. 8–9.
48. *Ibid.*, p. 88.
49. *New York,* p. 234.
50. *The Confessions of Claud,* Boston, 1887.
51. *Ibid.*, pp. 7–8.
52. *Ibid.*, p. 48.
53. *Ibid.*, p. 27.
54. *Ibid.*, p. 104.
55. *Ibid.*, pp. 331.
56. *Ibid.*, pp. 198–99.
57. *Ibid.*, p. 394.
58. *Ibid.*, pp. 344–45.

Chapter Six

1. For a discussion of these American literary concerns, see my article, "Some Forces in the Shaping of American Literature," *Tulane Studies in English,* XIV (1965), 97–108.

2. Charles Brockden Brown, *Ormond,* ed. Ernest Marchand (New York, 1937), pp. 3–4.

3. D. H. Lawrence, *Studies in Classic American Literature* (New York, 1923), pp. 5–7.

4. The comments in these letters are to Hayne, August 6, 1876; to Hayne, April 27, 1880; to Miss Whiting, April 5, 189?; and to Hayne, January 6, 1882. The excerpt from the letter to Miss Whiting is printed courtesy the Boston Public Library.

5. William Dean Howells, review of *A Gentleman of Leisure*, *Atlantic Monthly*, XLVIII (October, 1881), 564.

6. Review of *A Gentleman of Leisure*, *New York Times* (July 10, 1881), p. 10.

7. Review of *An Ambitious Woman*, *Nation*, XXXVIII (February 28, 1884), 194.

8. Review of *Tinkling Cymbals*, *New York Times* (June 22, 1884), p. 5.

9. Fawcett letter to Hayne, September 22, 1875.

10. Fawcett letter to Hayne, October 10, 1877.

11. Fawcett letter to Wyman, March 10, 1890, printed courtesy the Chicago Historical Society.

12. *A Gentleman of Leisure* (Boston, 1881), pp. 271–72.

13. *A Hopeless Case*, pp. 67–68.

14. *Fabian Dimitry* (Chicago, 1890), p. 65.

15. *A Gentleman of Leisure*, p. 156.

16. *Rutherford*, New York, 1894.

17. *Ibid.*, p. 15.

18. *Ibid.*, p. 33.

19. *Ibid.*, p. 46.

20. *Ibid.*, p. 94.

21. *Ibid.*, p. 189.

22. *Ibid.*, p. 82.

23. *Ibid.*, pp. 22–23.

24. *Ibid.*, pp. 30–32.

25. *Ibid.*, pp. 34–35.

26. *American Push*, Chicago, 1892.

27. *Ibid.*, p. 63.

28. *Ibid.*, p. 130.

29. *Ibid.*, p. 202.

30. *The Vulgarians*, New York, 1903.

31. The manuscript of *An Innocent Anglomaniac* is in my possession; it has never appeared in print, but it, too, like *The Pride of Intellect*, was probably written early in 1904. See Chapter 1, fn. 14.

32. *The Pride of Intellect;* see Chapter 1, fn. 14.

33. *Ibid.*, p. 270.

34. *Ibid.*, pp. 269–70.

35. *Ibid.*, p. 268.

36. See pp. 11–12 and Chapter 1, fn. 12.

Chapter Seven

1. The chief critical complaint was with Fawcett's stilted diction

and his turgid style. "Too much elaboration for the thought," the *Nation* said of *Fantasy and Passion* (May 16, 1878, p. 328). In its review of *Song and Story,* six years later, the *Nation* again noted that "the want of simplicity . . . seems likely always to prove his [Fawcett's] bane" (December 18, p. 528). The *New York Times* concurred: "His [Fawcett's] choice of adjectives as well as his reckless profusion of them carry his verse so near to the verge of bathos that it needs much good-will not to tumble over and have one's laugh out" (October 26, 1884, p. 6). There were some critics who appreciated Fawcett's poetry, but they too, found fault with his inflated style. The reviewer for *Harper's New Monthly Magazine* noted, for example, the "great force and beauty" and the "ripe and versatile imagination" of Fawcett's narrative poetry in *Song and Story,* but he still insisted that "the perfection of all these poems is marred by a grandiloquence of style which recalls the bombastic mouthings against which Shakespeare directed the battery of his raillery in the persons of Malvolio, Sir John Falstaff, and honest Nick Bottom" (1884, p. 967).

2. "A Few Literary Experiences," *Lippincott's Monthly Magazine,* XXXVII (1886), 415.

3. Review of *Song and Story, New York Times* (October 26, 1884), p. 6.

4. Review of *Songs of Doubt and Dream, Dial,* XV (July 16, 1893), 42.

5. Review of *Fantasy and Passion, Harper's New Monthly Magazine,* LVII (1878), 469.

6. "Edgar Fawcett," *National Cyclopaedia of American Biography,* VII (New York, 1897), 191.

7. Fawcett letter to Julian Hawthorne August 21, no year. The excerpt from this letter is printed courtesy the Berg Collection of the New York Public Library.

8. Fawcett letter to Hayne, September 9, 1876.

9. William Dean Howells, review of *Fantasy and Passion, Atlantic Monthly,* XLI (May, 1878), 632.

10. Richard Henry Stoddard, *Poet's Homes* (Boston, 1879), p. 77.

11. *Short Poems for Short People,* New York, 1872.

12. "A Sad Case," *ibid.,* p. 18.

13. "Above all Price," *Short Poems for Short People,* p. 20.

14. "Two Worlds," *Romance and Revery* (Boston, 1886), p. 67.

15. "Temptation," *ibid.,* p. 153.

16. Fawcett letter to Hayne, November 20, 1875.

17. "Darkness," *Fantasy and Passion* (Boston, 1878), p. 64.

18. Fawcett letter to Hayne, December 8, 1874.

19. "Fire," *Fantasy and Passion,* p. 129.

20. Fawcett letter to Hayne, September 22, 1875.

21. "Baudelaire," *Fantasy and Passion,* p. 191.

22. "Water-Lilies," *ibid.,* p. 16.

23. Robert G. Ingersoll, Prologue to Edgar Fawcett's *Agnosticism and Other Essays* (New York, 1889), pp. 7–8.

24. "A Kind of Preacher," *Romance and Revery,* pp. 52–53.

25. Ingersoll, "Prologue," *Agnosticism and Other Essays,* pp. 21–23.

26. "In the Year Ten Thousand," *Songs of Doubt and Dream* (New York, 1891), pp. 51–52.

27. Ingersoll, p. 8.

28. "A Dialogue," *Songs of Doubt and Dream,* p. 133.

29. "Herbert Spencer," *Fantasy and Passion,* p. 189.

30. "Poverty," *Romance and Revery,* pp. 72–75.

31. "Nature in Bondage," *Song and Story, Later Poems* (Boston, 1884), pp. 129–30.

32. A late eighteenth-century Quaker Cassandra, Woolman was distressed by early manifestations of material corruption in this country, and he prophesied the death of the American ideal of democratic equality.

33. "The Bartholdi Statue (Unveiled on Bedloe's Island, October 28, 1886)," *Songs of Doubt and Dream,* pp. 2 and 4.

Selected Bibliography

PRIMARY SOURCES

1. Essays—
Agnosticism and Other Essays. New York: Belford, Clarke and Company, 1889.
For Novelists and Poets. Copyright, March 6, 1888.*
How a Novel Is Written. Copyright, November 20, 1888.

2. Novels—
The Adopted Daughter. Chicago: F. T. Neely, 1892.
The Adventures of a Widow. Boston: James R. Osgood, 1884.
An Ambitious Woman. Boston: Houghton Mifflin and Company, 1884.
American Push. Chicago: F. J. Schulte and Company, 1892.
An Anonymous Letter. Copyright, March 4, 1891.
Asses Ears. New York: G. W. Carleton and Company, 1871.
B. B. Romance. New York: E. S. Werner, 1912.
The Best Match in Town. Copyright, March 14, 1895.
The Bond of Flesh. Copyright, March 10, 1892.
Cheviot's Last Chance. Copyright, November 12, 1888.
Comedy of Counterplots. Copyright, November 16, 1894.
The Confessions of Claud. Boston: Ticknor and Company, 1887.
A Daughter of Silence. New York: Belford Company, 1890.
A Dead Man's Vengeance. Copyright, July 17, 1889.
A Demoralizing Marriage. Philadelphia: J. B. Lippincott Company, 1889.
The Destruction of the Moon. Copyright, February 5, 1892.
Divided Lives. Chicago: Belford, Clarke and Company, 1888.
Dorothy Dillow. Copyright, February 1, 1893.
Douglas Duane. Philadelphia: J. B. Lippincott Company, 1888.
Ellen Story. New York: E. J. Hale and Son, 1876.
The Evil That Men Do. New York: Belford Company, 1889.
Fabian Dimitry. Chicago: Rand, McNally and Company, 1890.
The False Friend. New York: George Munro, 1880.
Frankie and His Kindred. Copyright, August 22, 1887.

---

*I have included here Fawcett's works that were copyrighted, but never published. The list may prove of value to those interested in future research.

A Gentleman of Leisure. Boston: Houghton Mifflin and Company, 1881.
The Ghost of Guy Thyrle. New York: Peter Fenelon Collier, 1895.
An Heir to Millions. Chicago: F. J. Schulte and Company, 1892.
Her Fair Fame. New York: Merrill and Baker, 1894.
Her Statue. Copyright, November 14, 1893.
His Only Child. Copyright, May 2, 1888.
A Hopeless Case. Boston: Houghton Mifflin and Company, 1880.
The House at High Bridge. Boston: Ticknor and Company, 1887.
How a Husband Forgave. New York: Belford Company, 1890.
An Innocent Anglomaniac. Manuscript, 1904.
Life's Fitful Fever, Being the Memoirs of Clarence Disoway Torrington. New York: Peter Fenelon Collier, 1896.
Loaded Dice. New York: Tait, Sons and Company, 1893.
A Lost Day. Copyright, April 9, 1891.
Man from Mars. Copyright, June 3, 1891.
A Man's Will. New York: Funk and Wagnalls, 1888.
Mark's Mother. Copyright, July 28, 1893.
A Martyr of Destiny. New York: Peter Fenelon Collier, 1894.
A Mild Barbarian. New York: D. Appleton and Company, 1894.
Mildred Allaire. Copyright, July 9, 1884.
Miriam Balestier. Chicago: Belford, Clarke and Company, 1888.
Mrs. Thorndyke's Conscience. Copyright, March 10, 1885.
My Day of Doom. Copyright, September 11, 1896.
The New Nero. New York: Peter Fenelon Collier, 1893.
New York. New York: F. Tennyson Neely, 1898.
A New York Family. New York: Caswell Publishing Company, 1891.
Olivia Delaplaine. Boston: Ticknor and Company, 1888.
Outrageous Fortune. New York: The Concord Press, 1894.
A Portrait Painter. Copyright, January 6, 1893.
The Pride of Intellect. Michigan State University Dissertation, 1964.
Purple and Fine Linen. New York: G. W. Carleton and Company, 1873.
Revenge or Pardon. Which? Copyright, September 11, 1896.
A Romance of Old New York. Philadelphia: J. B. Lippincott Company, 1897.
A Romance of Two Brothers. New York: Minerva Publishing Company, 1891.
Rutherford. New York: Funk and Wagnalls, 1884.
Social Silhouettes. Boston: Ticknor and Company, 1885.
Solarion, Philadelphia: J. B. Lippincott Company, 1889.
A Special Providence. Copyright, September 11, 1896.
A Stormy Night. Copyright, July 6, 1893.

A Story of Two Cousins. Copyright, February 10, 1885.
The Tale of Two Misers. Copyright, September 28, 1891.
Tinkling Cymbals. Boston: James R. Osgood and Company, 1884.
Two Daughters of One Race. Philadelphia: J. B. Lippincott Company, 1897.
The Vulgarians. New York: The Smart Set Publishing Company, 1903.
Was It a Ghost? Copyright, May 12, 1885.
Women Must Weep. Chicago: Laird and Lee, 1891.

3. Plays—(date and place of first production in parentheses)
Americans Abroad. (Daly's Theater, New York, October 5, 1881.)
The Earl. (Hollis Street Theater, Boston, April 11, 1887.)
A False Friend. (Union Square Theater, New York, June 21, 1880.)
Sixes and Sevens. (Bijou Opera House, New York, March, 1881.)
Our First Families. (Daly's Theater, September 23, 1880.)

4. Poetry—
Blooms and Brambles. London: Elliot Stock, 1889.
Fantasy and Passion. Boston: Roberts Brothers, 1878.
Romance and Revery. Boston: Ticknor and Company, 1886.
Short Poems for Short People. New York: Francis B. Felt and Company, 1872.
Song and Story, Later Poems. Boston: James R. Osgood and Company, 1884.
Songs of Doubt and Dream. New York: Funk and Wagnalls, 1891.
Voices and Visions, Later Years. London: Eveleigh Nash, 1903.

5. Verse Drama—
The Buntling Ball. New York: Funk and Wagnalls, 1884.
The New King Arthur. New York: Funk and Wagnalls, 1885.

6. Fawcett's Poetry and Prose in Periodicals
"Allegory," *Century*, XLV (April, 1893), 891.
"American Impression of the New Grub Street," *Bookman*, XII (October, 1900), 129–32.
"American in England," *Munsey's Magazine*, XXIX (April, 1903), 40.
"Antitheses," *Century*, XLVII (February, 1894), 639.
"Aux Invalides," *Century*, XLI (March, 1891), 696.
"Baudelaire," *Atlantic Monthly*, XXXVI (December, 1875), 703.
"Bizarrerie," *Lippincott's Monthly Magazine*, LXXIII (April, 1904), 512.
"Dead World," *Century*, XLI (February, 1891), 498.

"Doreen," *Lippincott's Monthly Magazine,* LXXIII (January, 1904), 3–72.

"Extravaganza," *Munsey's Magazine,* XXVIII (November, 1902), 195.

"A Few Literary Experiences," *Lippincott's Monthly Magazine,* XXXVII (1886), 412–17.

"Grapes," *Atlantic Monthly,* XXXVI (November, 1875), 602–3.

"Harp of My Heart," *Lippincott's Monthly Magazine,* LXXI (March, 1903), 382.

"Immortelles," *Atlantic Monthly,* XXXV (April, 1875), 407.

"In the Year Ten Thousand," *Arena,* I (February, 1890), 247–52.

"International Sweethearts," *New England Magazine,* XXVI (April, 1902), 152–66.

"Lincoln Loquitur," *Poet Lore,* XI (October, 1899), 258.

"Literature and the Drama," *Dial,* XIV (January, 1893), 38–40.

"Love in Masquerade," *Century,* XLVIII (August, 1894), 558.

"Minorchord," *Century,* XLVIII (May, 1894), 15.

"Nathan Hale," *Reader,* IV (June, 1904), 100–101.

"One Touch of Nature," *Century,* XLV (March, 1893), 759.

"Paradise of Gamblers," *Arena,* IV (November, 1891), 641–51.

"Pavement Pictures," *Century,* XLIV (October, 1892), 845.

"Pawnbroker," *Century,* XLI (November, 1890), 32.

"Plutocracy and Snobbery in New York," *Arena,* IV (July, 1891), 142–51.

"Oediphus and the Sphinx," *North American Review,* CLXXV (December, 1902), 871–76.

"Prig," *Century,* XLVI (May, 1893), 158.

"Queen Christina and de Liar," *Arena,* II (June, 1890), 1–8.

"Resurrection of Edith," *Lippincott's Monthly Magazine,* LXXI (January, 1903), 85–94.

"Retrospect," *Nation,* LIV (March, 1892), 254.

"Should Critics Be Gentlemen?," *Lippincott's Monthly Magazine* XXXIX (1887), 163–77.

"Sleep and Death," *Independent,* LII (February, 1900), 303.

"Spring Days in Venice," *Cosmopolitan,* XXX (April, 1901), 613–22.

"Stronger than Death," *Munsey's Magazine,* XXIX (June, 1903), 443.

"To Robert G. Ingersoll," *Arena,* IX (December, 1893), 114–17.

"Traffic," *Century,* XLIV (July, 1892), 384.

"Unpardonable Sin," *Munsey's Magazine,* XXVIII (January, 1903), 492–505.

"Waste," *Atlantic Monthly,* XXXV (June, 1875), 683.

"Woes of the New York Working-Girl," *Arena,* V (December, 1891), 26–35.

7. Location of Fawcett Manuscripts

Buffalo Public Library: "Irony," "My Echo," "Sister Dorothy"; Chicago Historical Society: "A City Eclogue," "A Dead World," "What to Read in Summer"; Duke University Library: "Art," "Barca-rolle," "Eternity," "Fabrics," "From a Lover," "From a Madhouse," "He and She," "Hypocrites," "Keats," "The Meeting," "Le Revers de la Medaille," "To Paul Hamilton Hayne," "Whittier," "Will It Be Strong?"; Harvard University Library: "The Dominick Diamonds," "Nature in Bondage," "Some City Days"; Henry E. Huntington Library and Art Gallery: "Married Bohemians"; New York Public Library: "A Tuberose"; Trinity College Library: "A White Camellia"; University of Virginia Library: "The Punishment"; Yale University Library: "Bigotry," "Lilacs," "The Twilight of the Poets"; Private Collection of Stanley R. Harrison: "Brenda," "Christine," "Dorothy Vanderveer," "A Heart's History," "The Icicle," *An Innocent Anglo-maniac*, "Lady Meadowmere's Method," "Oceanview," *The Pride of Intellect*, "The Unpardonable Sin."

SECONDARY SOURCES

1. Reviews of Fawcett's Works[*]
"The Adventures of a Widow," *Nation*, XXXIX (October 9, 1884), 314.
"An Ambitious Woman," *Atlantic Monthly*, LIII (May, 1884), 710–11. *Nation*, XXXVIII (February 28, 1884), 194. *New York Times* (December 17, 1883), p. 3.
"A Demoralizing Marriage," *Critic*, XI (April 6, 1889), 167.
"Divided Lives," *Critic*, XI (January 26, 1889), 40.
"Ellen Story," *Harper's New Monthly Magazine*, LIII (1876), 629.
"Fantasy and Passion," *Atlantic Monthly*, XLI (May, 1878), 632–35. *Harper's New Monthly Magazine*, LVII (1878), 469. *Nation*, XXVI (May 16, 1878), 328. *Scribner's Monthly Magazine* (June 1878), 296–98.
"A Gentleman of Leisure," *Atlantic Monthly*, XLVIII (October, 1881), 561–64. *New York Times* (July 10, 1881), p. 10.
"A Hopeless Case," *Atlantic Monthly*, XLVI (September, 1880), 415–16. *New York Times* (June 27, 1880), p. 10.
"The House at High Bridge," *Dial*, VII (December, 1886), 189–90.
"A Man's Will," *Nation*, XLVI (June 28, 1888), 530. *New York Times* (July 22, 1888), p. 10.
"A Mild Barbarian," *New York Times* (October 14, 1894), p. 27.

[*]Annotation would be repetitive, since the cited reviews have previously been alluded to in the study proper.

"Miriam Balestier," *Critic*, XI (March 23, 1889), 142–43.
"The New King Arthur," *Critic*, V (February 6, 1886), 68–69. *Nation*, XLI (December 24, 1885), 541.
"New York," *Independent*, LI (January 26, 1899), 280–81. *New York Times* (October 8, 1898), p. 662. *New York Times* (January 28, 1899), p. 64.
"A New York Family," *Catholic World*, LV (July, 1891), 599–600. *Critic*, XV (June 27, 1891), 335.
"Purple and Fine Linen," *Nation*, XVII (July 10, 1873), 27.
"A Romance of Old New York," *New York Times* (May 1, 1897), pp. 3–4.
"Rutherford," *New York Times* (August 23, 1884), p. 3.
"Social Silhouettes," *Athenaeum*, reprinted in the *Critic*, V (January 23, 1886), 48.
"Song and Story," *Critic and Good Literature* (September 6, 1884), 119. *Harper's New Monthly Magazine*, LXIX (1884), 966–67. *Nation*, XXXIX (December 18, 1884), 528. *New York Times* (October 26, 1884), p. 6.
"Songs of Doubt and Dream," *Dial*, XV (July 16, 1893), 42.
"Tinkling Cymbals," *Lippincott's Monthly Magazine*, XXXIV (August, 1884), 215–16. *Nation*, XXXIX (July 31, 1884), 96. *New York Times* (June 22, 1884), p. 5.
"Women Must Weep," *New York Times* (February 14* 1892), p. 19.

2. Studies

HARRISON, STANLEY R. "Through a Nineteenth-Century Looking Glass: The Letters of Edgar Fawcett," *Tulane Studies in English*, XV (1967), 107–57. Excerpts from Fawcett's letters are gathered under the names of the authors he commented upon in his correspondences. The letters shed light upon Fawcett's literary views and upon the late nineteenth-century literary fraternity.

————. "Edgar Fawcett, A Minor Writer in the Literary Current of His Time: an Edition of His Unpublished Novel, *The Pride of Intellect*, unpublished doctoral dissertation, Michigan State University, 1964. The dissertation establishes Fawcett as a popular writer of his time, suggests the influences that shaped his works, and speculates upon the nature and extent of his influence upon other writers. It also presents an edition of his unpublished novel, *The Pride of Intellect*, and a collection of his letters to literary personages.

RIDEING, WILLIAM H. "Edgar Fawcett," *Bookman*, XXXII (December, 1910), 436–39. The article is a reminiscence, written six

years after Fawcett's death. Rideing recalls the creative intensity that was the mark of Fawcett, and he comments sadly upon the diminishing nature of Fawcett's literary reputation.
STODDARD, RICHARD H. *Poet's Homes.* Boston: J. R. Osgood and Company, 1879. In the one chapter Stoddard devotes to Fawcett, he reveals some of Fawcett's personal traits and comments favorably upon his poetry.

Index

(The works of Fawcett are listed under his name)